Shaman, Jhankri & Néle
Music Healers of Indigenous Cultures

Written and Produced by
Pat Moffitt Cook

Foreword by
Julian Burger Ph.D.

Shaman, Jhankri & Néle

Music Healers of Indigenous Cultures

Written and Produced by
Pat Moffitt Cook

Project Director
Russell Charno D.C.

Executive Producer
Jeffrey Charno

Editor
Helen Zelon

Graphic Design and Production
Joanna Jaeger

©1997 Ellipsis Arts...
All rights reserved

No part of this book may be used or reproduced in any manner whatsoever without permission except in the case of brief quotations embodied in critical articles and reviews.

For information or a catalog:
Ellipsis Arts...
P.O. Box 305
Roslyn, New York 11576
phone: (800)788-6670
fax: (516)621-2750
e-mail: elliarts@aol.com

Table of Contents

Foreword ~~~~~~~~~~~~~~~4
By Julian Burger Ph.D.

Introduction ~~~~~~~~~~~~~~6
By Pat Moffitt Cook

1. Babaji ~~~~~~~~~~~~~~~8
North Indian Ojha

2. Koshalya ~~~~~~~~~~~~12
Hindu Village Healer

3. Ram Tmapa & Suni Ram ~~~~~~18
Jhankri of Nepal

4. Don Agustin Rivas-Vasquez ~~23
Peruvian Ayahuasca Shaman

5. Micheline Forestal~~~~~~~~~28
Haitian Vodou Manbo

6. Kanucas Littlefish ~~~~~~~~32
Native American Anishnabe Medicine Man

7. Maestro Demosdenes Ramirez Hurtas~34
Kuna Indian Song Healer of the San Blas Islands

8. Darkiking Don Alejandro ~~~~38
Amazon Medicine Man

9. Alexander Tavakay ~~~~~~~44
Tuvan Shaman

10. Pointing Father ~~~~~~~~~47
Spiritual Baptist Immigrants from Saint Vincent Island

11. Mara'akame~~~~~~~~~~~50
Huichol Peyote Shaman from Mexico

12. Jorge K'in ~~~~~~~~~~~~56
Lacandon Mayan Healer

13. Néle Buna Inayenikidili ~~~~62
Kuna Indian Seer of the San Blas Islands

14. Anselmo Palma Cruz ~~~~~~69
Tarahumara Owiruame from The Sierra Madres

15. Kangsinmu ~~~~~~~~~~~~76
Spirit-Possessed Shaman of Korea

16. Steve Old Coyote~~~~~~~~~80
"Road Man" of the Native American Church

17. Simon Eliet ~~~~~~~~~~~84
Inatulele from Panama

18. Phawo Nyidhon ~~~~~~~~~88
Tibetan Oracle

CD Track Listing ~~~~~~~~~~~92

Photo Credits ~~~~~~~~~~~~93

References~~~~~~~~~~~~~~94

Acknowledgments ~~~~~~~~~~95

Biography ~~~~~~~~~~~~~~96

Foreword

by Julian Burger Ph.D.

"The health of the people begins with the Creator, then transforms to Natural Laws which then become our obligation to fulfill. The Creator gave us Natural Laws and spiritual beliefs for our protection and to help us maintain our health and wellness. For every right, there is a responsibility. We cannot have one without the other. These laws govern all our relations which mean the whole of the earth including the sun, moon, stars, sky, wind and rain. We believe we are a part of the whole Creation and not separated from it. We are part of the cycle of nature whose laws are timeless and unchangeable. Native laws are based on natural law in that our institutions are designed to flow with nature rather than subdue or control it."

Chief Germaine Tremmel,
Lakota Nation
Speaking at the fourteenth session of the
United Nations Working Group on
Indigenous Populations, July 1996.

Many people who read this book and listen to the words and music captured on the CDs and audio tapes will have little or no knowledge of the lives and cultures of the peoples which inspired them. Perhaps some listeners may have watched a documentary or traveled to a country where traditional dances and songs are part of a larger programme of sun and sea and good food — a hard-earned rest for a year or a lifetime of work. You may think that these indigenous cultures are disappearing, eroded by the force of our own dynamic, hungry, all-encompassing global view of the future. We might feel sympathy and we might experience sadness. We should not. The peoples who tell their stories here are among the most resilient. They have endured despite the unwelcome experience of colonization and a continuing dispossession of their lands and resources. They need not our sympathy, but our understanding, respect and solidarity.

The World's indigenous peoples are enjoying a cultural and political renaissance. Increasingly, their distinctive ways of life are recognized and celebrated and their contributions to the history, cultures and sciences of the countries in which they live are being acknowledged. This is in marked contrast to twenty or thirty years ago, when most State policies were based on the premise that indigenous people would eventually be assimilated into mainstream societies. The demands by indigenous people for recognition of their right to determine their own development and futures and for land are at long last being heard if not always realized. At the United Nations there is progress also. Governments have before them a draft declaration on the rights of indigenous peoples which, when it is reviewed and adopted by the General Assembly, will set a framework for relations between States and indigenous people. In 1993, the World Body celebrated the international Year of the World's Indigenous People. Recently, the World Body proclaimed an international Decade of the World's Indigenous People for the years 1995 to 2004 as part of a challenge to the international community to put an end to the disadvantage that indigenous people often face in areas such as health, housing, education and development.

As we move towards the new millennium, one welcome development is the new respect which is being accorded the voice of indigenous peoples. Their message is at long last reaching out to more people. It calls for our understanding that we are temporary guardians of the earth which we inherit from our lives. It challenges notions of homogeneity and acclaims cultural diversity. It argues above all for the right of all peoples to enjoy the freedom to choose their own future for themselves and their children.

The health of the indigenous peoples and their society is a core concern. The statistics for life expectancy, child morbidity and preventable diseases are almost universally below the average of the populations in the countries in which they live. The reasons are complex enough: bad nutrition, poverty, and the vulnerability that accompanies the breakdown of once proud and independent peoples. Modern medicine has been welcomed and indigenous people have been, on the whole, its beneficiaries. But Western drugs, medical technology and expertise have not solved the deeper problems of indigenous society nor fully restored the health of its people. As one distinguished Australian Aboriginal person has commented, "Health cannot be brought into an indigenous community on the back of a truck."

The health of indigenous peoples cannot be separated from the health of the environment or the recognition of indigenous peoples to take back control of their fixtures. Nor can health be considered apart from the wider context of indigenous culture. Sheila Watt-Cloutier of the Inuit Circumpolar Conference has stated: "Health, we can safely say, is not just the absence of disease. It is in fact a delicate balance of one's physical, emotional and spiritual well-being."

We should be grateful for the work carried out by the author and producers of "Shaman, Jhankri and Néle: Music Healers of Indigenous Cultures." They present an extraordinary World to us. The texts, the music and the words of the healers help us to comprehend the "delicate balance" that characterizes the indigenous concept of health. They are showing that there are other sciences, other ways of understanding and other ways of knowing. They are recording an important treasure and helping us to open our minds and hearts. Indigenous healers have other ways of seeing and of curing.

There is a cautionary footnote to add. As we listen and learn about the approaches to health that are taken by the different indigenous healers whose practices are reviewed in this book and CD, we would do well to recall that we are being introduced to sciences and religions often older than our own, not simply hearing folkloric tales. We are privileged listeners, for much of what is being shared is sacred and if traditional healers reveal this knowledge it is in the form of a trust.

We have often dismissed what we do not understand. In health matters, many of us have an almost blind faith in modern high-tech medicine. But the course of Western medicine is fairly well littered with quack cures which obtained comprehensive approval from the medical establishment. There is nothing sacrosanct about our modern health sciences. Nor should we forget the enormous debt which modern medicine owes to traditional healers and cures. Many of modern medical successes owe something to so-called traditional health practices. Unfortunately, and to our discredit, too often that debt goes unrecognized.

As we read and listen, we can perhaps allow our minds and hearts to open and wonder about some of the mysteries of the world and of the knowledge and visions which give its richness and diversity.

Julian Burger Ph.D. is responsible for the Indigenous Programme within the office of the United Nations High Commissioner for Human Rights and the Center for Human Rights. The Programme focuses on facilitating indigenous peoples' access to the United Nations and deepening public understanding of indigenous cultures and aspirations as well as on ensuring that their human rights are respected. He is also the secretary of the United Nations Working Group on Indigenous Populations and the Commission on Human Rights working group on the draft declaration on the rights of Indigenous peoples. Julian Burger is the author of several books and many articles about indigenous peoples.

Introduction  by Pat Moffitt Cook

Sound Is Sacred

Sound is sacred. In all religious and spiritual traditions sound, word and music are instrumental in creating and sustaining the universe, nature and humankind. Healing sounds are part of a "sacred therapy" still practiced among holy men and women, shamans and healers and the indigenous peoples of the earth. The common belief that vibration permeates all things, seen and unseen, forms the foundation of an ancient science and practice of healing with music.

Throughout the ages, by trial and error, selected sounds and rhythms developed into tools and remedies for diagnosing and curing illness. Sophisticated breathing patterns evolved together with prayerful chants and sacred healing songs. The songs cure, petition benevolent deities, invite spirit possession, and induce states of ecstasy. This ancient sound therapy is still practiced today. It holds fast to spiritual roots, echoing a legacy that possesses a profound knowledge of how sound and music assist in healing the human psyche and spirit.

It has been a long journey to the sonic actualization of prayer and medicinal songs. Every generation within each culture contributed to the evolution of these sound methods and compositions. The indigenous music healers are "living treasures," links to the past, and masterful psychologists and physicians. Like their ancestors they use sound as a primary gateway to inner consciousness, freedom from pain and transcendence. Their sacred musical prescriptions intercept the course of illness and remind those people sick in body and mind how to function in balance once again.

As a practitioner and educator in the field of music in health care, I became aware of the potential of traditional healing music as an area of research while traveling, living and studying music-centered healing practices in Southeast Asia, India, Nepal, Japan and North and Central America. For two decades, I have witnessed and participated in the "creative" and "soulful" exchange between doctor and patient, shaman and spirit, healer and disease, through music. This passionate display of care for another human being, often without payment, has left an indelible impression on my mind and heart.

The practice of music in healing among indigenous peoples has been revealed through scholarly studies in ethnomusicology, medical anthropology, mythology, history and religion. The importance of music, as a part of traditional medical technology, is undeniable. Its very existence confirms and inspires contemporary theories and practices in sound and music-centered therapies today. This history motivates research and provides a foundation for the development of new paradigms in the emerging field of music in healing in contemporary health care.

These sound and music repertoires are fast disappearing. After centuries of basic research vast storehouses of indigenous knowledge are vanishing, due largely in part to Western modernization. The process of culture-change is accelerating at unprecedented rates throughout the world. The opportunity to document, study, and gain insight first hand, from living traditions, is momentous. Proof of this can be seen and felt by botanists, herbalists, ethnopharmacologists, practitioners in traditional and alternative medicine, nutritionists and by different ailing populations who benefit from complimentary and organic-related treatment. Samples of medicinal plants for either replication in the pharmaceutical lab or for natural reproduction are disappearing along with the rain forests, and other natural vegetation locales. This same dilemma is true for traditional healing systems that employ music. Change is inevitable, and knowing this we are prompted to learn more about the endangered elements in society and nature.

Indigenous sound healers reserve their healing-music repertoires for sickness, pain, spiritual and physical death and to mediate between god and nature — never for entertainment. If the Huichol *mara'akame* (shaman) petitions a deity without reason the god becomes angry and could distrust future requests for aid. The Kuna *néle* (seer) in the San Blas islands will not charge the *nuchus* (medicine dolls) without the need for their *kurgin* (power) in diagnosing illness. The Hindu village *ojha* (healer) does not invoke *Sitla* (the goddess of disease and small pox) without a purpose; Sitla brings disease as easily as she takes it away.

Healing-music repertoires are rare and sacred possessions. They are not easily shared with outsiders. Even traveling to remote parts of India, Tibet, Nepal or Northern Mexico does not guarantee the traveler an opportunity to witness or participate in a healing session. As a result, there are few authentic field recordings available. This is one reason scholarly research has not focused on it in the past. Only recently, prompted by ecological concerns, new interests in Western sound healing and the fact that indigenous wisdom is disappearing, are steps being taken to uncover and preserve ancient traditions.

It is with great skepticism, hope and ultimately trust in the Divine that the indigenous healers represented in this book, share their knowledge, lives and healing music with you. It is my hope that this tremendous act of trust on their behalf helps to quicken the process of preservation and increases public awareness and respect for the indigenous peoples of the earth.

In the following chapters you will meet an *ojha*, *maestro*, *néle*, *manbo*, *phawo*, *jhankri*, *ayahuascero*, *kangsinmu*, shamans and other musical doctors. After reading their stories, the accompanying CD will provide a listening experience of the actual healing music. Each recording has its own unique quality and purpose. It is important to keep in mind that this music was not created to entertain but to stimulate an effect in their patients. Most recordings were made in the last six years with the exception of the Huichol mara'akame that was recorded in the Sierra Madre mountains in 1940.

This project bridges the gap, links the past with the present, serves to some extent as documentation and clarification of indigenous methods, healers, sacred healing musical instruments and actual sounds as well as stimulates a broader vision of the power of sound in healing. It also serves to increase the awareness of the general public and health care professionals alike of the value and rarity of indigenous sound healing. The masters of sound healing can tell us how music affects our minds, emotions and most of all (something missing in Western medicine) our souls. When we touch the sacred in us and reestablish a relationship with it, healing can occur. Sacred healing music repertoires can access this relationship.

Pat Moffitt Cook

CHAPTER ONE

Babaji
North Indian Ojha

Indian village healing practices, which are rooted in a spiritual rather than a microbiological concept of disease, can be traced to ancient Vedic texts, Hindu mythology, Indian mysticism and local folk traditions. Illness is most often attributed to demons, restless or angry ancestors, unrelated spirits who have died tragically and supreme deities who attack and possess individuals for divine reasons. As professor of religion David Kinsley put it, "Belief that possession causes a wide variety of human troubles, outrageous behavior, economic disasters and death, is widespread in India."

Village healers are also known as ghost healers. They negotiate directly with disease-causing ghosts through sound, silent mantras and song.

Ojhas

Two Hindu village healers I recently encountered are characteristic of a large class of healers in northern India. One, a man in his early forties, is named Babaji; the other is a woman, Koshalya, in her mid-sixties. They are called *ojhas* (healers).

Both healers belong to the third Indian caste. Numerous classes exist under this single social umbrella. Each one identifies individual social status and vocation. Babaji belongs to "Yadav" or the merchant class. Koshalya belongs to "Kurmi," the milkman class. Both ojhas are skilled in collecting and preparing mineral and herbal medicines, leading devotional and healing songs, reciting prayer and performing other aspects of sacred ritual. Their innate and developed intuitive abilities provide strength and psychotherapeutic counseling for their patients.

Babaji practices just north of Varanasi. He treats local villagers and the well-to-do from Bombay and Delhi, who either come to him or provide his transport to other locations. He is best known for curing the crippled and persons suffering from mental problems, ranging from mild depression to insanity.

Babaji

"I owned a small shop on the main street. Baba, the old healer, wanted to teach me secret songs and how to prepare medicines. He said I was an ojha."

"I prayed to the goddess for direction. She came upon me, 'Close your shop and build a temple in this field. Fly a red flag from the roof. You will become an ojha. Do not worry about money or your family's needs.'"

> "I closed my shop the next day, and everything has come to be. I could not sing before and now I have a beautiful voice to heal with, a gift from the goddess!"
>
> *Babaji*

Above: Parvati, Hindu Goddess

Babaji

Babaji the ojha is well-known now. He is married and has two adolescent sons. Babaji dresses in a graying white cotton *kurta* and matching pajama-like pants. A checked blue and yellow woolen scarf helps keep him warm. His handsome face and smiling eyes welcome all who come to him for help.

On Tuesdays and Thursdays he receives the sick from his village and nearby cities. His charm and obvious compassion make him popular among his neighbors. Stories of his vocal resonance and miracle cures are legion.

The ojha's clinic (temple) stands inside a red brick-walled compound in a dusty field. Wooden double doors mark the entrance. Their blue paint bears the muddy hand prints of years of countless visitors.

Inside, a brick-lined corridor leads to an open-sky waiting room. Two religious shrines occupy the back wall, shielded from dust storms and summer downpours by a roof overhang. The shrine at the right, nestled deep within a red painted alcove, is for Hindus. It embraces *Siva,* the god of destruction, and *Parvati,* Siva's consort and supreme female deity. Pictures of *Durga,* the supreme female goddess and remover of obstacles, are scattered on the walls above the shrine.

The deep, spare alcove on the left is painted a brilliant turquoise and is reserved for people of the Muslim faith. A low fence symbolically warns women not to trespass. Although only two shrines are represented within the clinic compound, Babaji treats people of all faiths. "My teacher was a Muslim man, and I am Hindu by birth," said Babaji. "If a Hindu comes to me, I heal them in front of this Hindu shrine. I sing Hindu songs and chant Hindu names of god. If a Muslim comes to me I step over the fence, and treat those people."

Babaji at his Hindu alter.

The Healing Music

Babaji uses sacred words and names of gods and goddesses contained in chant-like melodies, repetitive rhythms and changing vocal dynamics. He induces dramatic exaggerated in-breaths, taken at specific times within the healing session. These inhalations deliver diagnostic and prescriptive information sent by *Sitla,* the goddess of disease. Silent mantras empowered by the deity then waft over the patient. This vibratory medicine overpowers the ghost that possesses the patient and intercepts the course of illness.

"All of my songs come directly from the goddess," says Babaji. "I sing a devotional song in the beginning to prepare myself and the patient. There must be an atmosphere of trust and devotion. When the goddess has come upon me I hear her song and see with her eyes."

When the preparation is complete, the patient is coaxed through sing-song dialogue to identify his or her illness. The voice of the patient is hesitant at first. Babaji describes, "The ghost blocks the voice. The patient cannot speak. The body shakes wildly; even his head hits the floor and turns quickly from side to side. This is the ghost resisting my treatment."

Babaji's song grows stronger, compelling the patient to respond. Finally, the patient sings out and identifies the disease. "When the ghost speaks, then I can make a diagnosis," says Babaji.

When the disease reveals itself, both patient and ojha are ready for the next step. Babaji's melody changes and modulates upward. New words, including those calling the disease (ghost) by name, are added. The patient's attention is continually directed towards the goddess in an effort to shift focus away from the hold of the possessing spirit, pain or mental stress.

Each stage of learned and improvisational music-making has a specific purpose in the healing process, and produces a different release. Each song formula received during the healing (from the goddess, via Babaji) is specific to the patient.

"The goddess told me to send my oldest son to medical school," Babaji told me. "When he opens his office he must fly the red flag from the roof. The power of the goddess Durga will be with him. He will be a very special doctor!"

Track 1
Babaji
"Song for Depression and Fatigue"
This song was excerpted from a recording of an actual treatment session for a man who was suffering from depression, fatigue and general ill health. It was recorded in Babaji's clinic in April of 1994.

CHAPTER TWO

Koshalya
HINDU VILLAGE HEALER

"Sitla came upon me. My eyes were closed. When they opened I saw strange things. Songs and words pounded in my head. For seven days and six nights the goddess lived in me. I stayed inside her temple. No one could touch me or I would scream. When Sitla left me I knew I was a healer. That was long ago. Now, with song I invite the goddess to come to my healing hut, to come upon me. Through her grace and power I heal people with jaundice and small pox and babies with fevers."

Koshalya

Koshalya's village is south of Varanasi. It is typical of most in North India. The contemporary world has not yet disturbed the peaceful pace of village life, and the roads are dusty and lined with grass or brick huts. The village is poor, but graced by surrounding *nim* trees and tall golden grasses that bend slightly in the breeze. Cowbells ring constantly, and cattle and water buffalo wander freely in the streets. The women dress in cotton saris and the men in plain white kurtas. Faces are dirty, and runny noses, insect bites and sores afflict the faces of children.

Small roadside stands displaying scant inventories of candy, chips, crackers and other sundries appear to be the only trade, except where men and women tend cows, vegetables, flowers — and children.

Koshalya was in her garden when we arrived. Her yellow cotton sari only partially covered her wrinkled skin and sagging breasts. She moved out of her garden with the grace and natural beauty of a person at one with the land. On each wrist she wore a common silver village bracelet. Her silver hair fell loosely below her shoulders. Her body was slender and muscular; her bearing was firm, energetic and direct. Tonight she would sing "healing songs" with the women of her village.

The love of the people for Koshalya was obvious. The village depends on her for their health and well-being. She is considered expert in curing blindness, smallpox, fever, infertility, jaundice, menstrual ailments and illness *(roji)* in general. She calls upon Sitla, local spirits *(yaksa)* and ancestral spirits *(pitris)* for assistance. Few in the village can

Above: Koshalya's altar

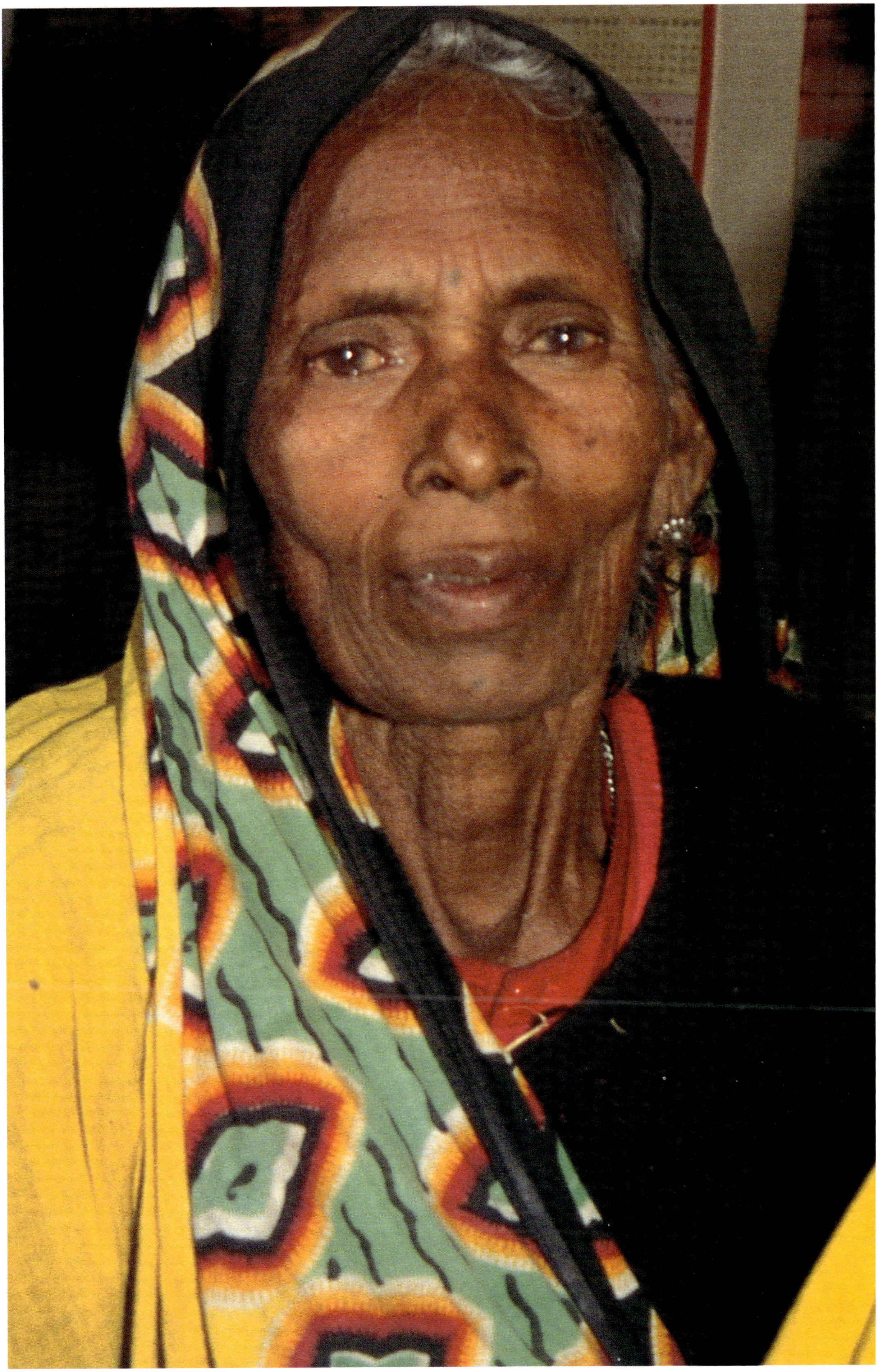

Koshalya

Koshalya with the village women sitting outside of her healing hut.

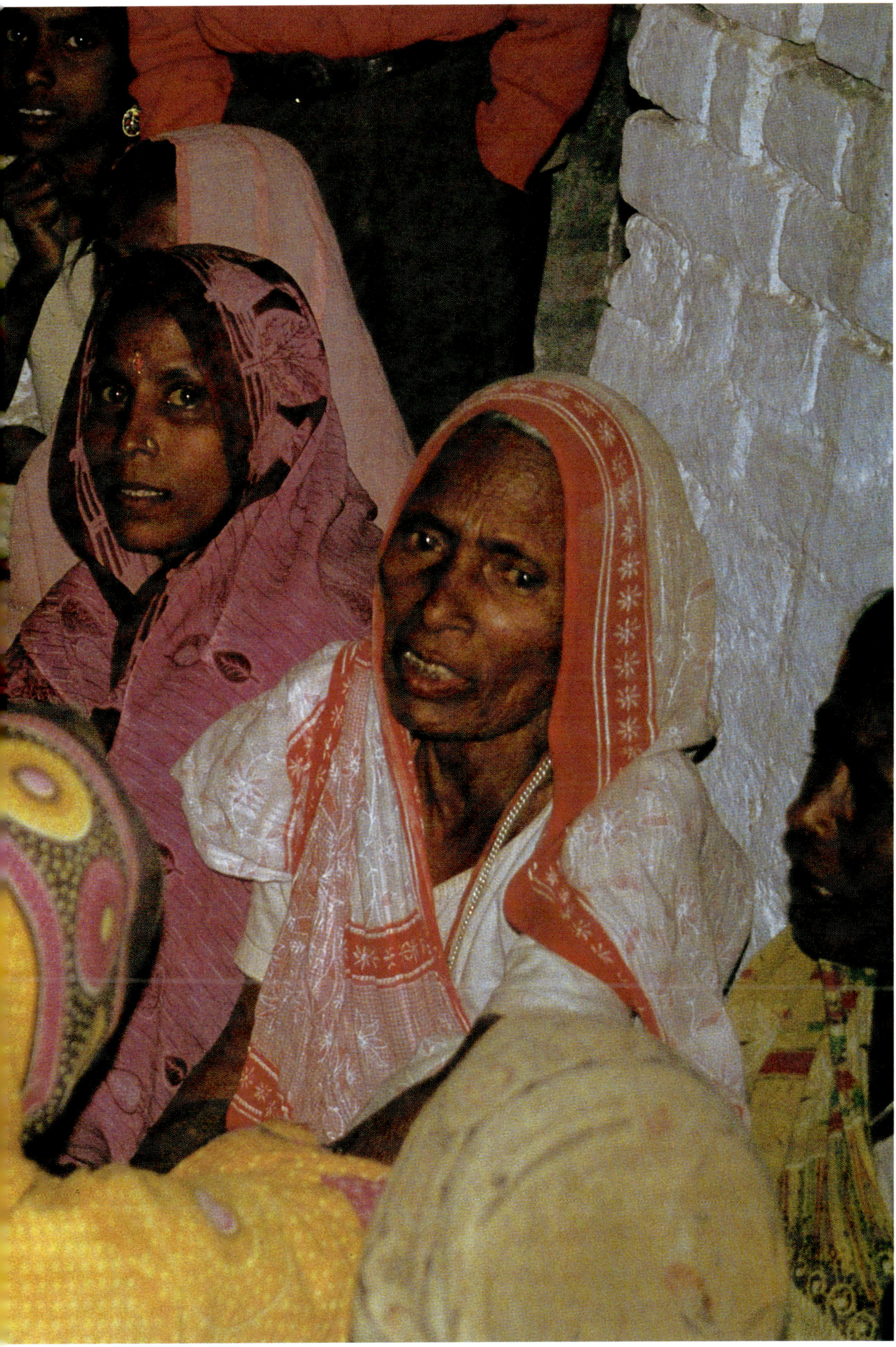

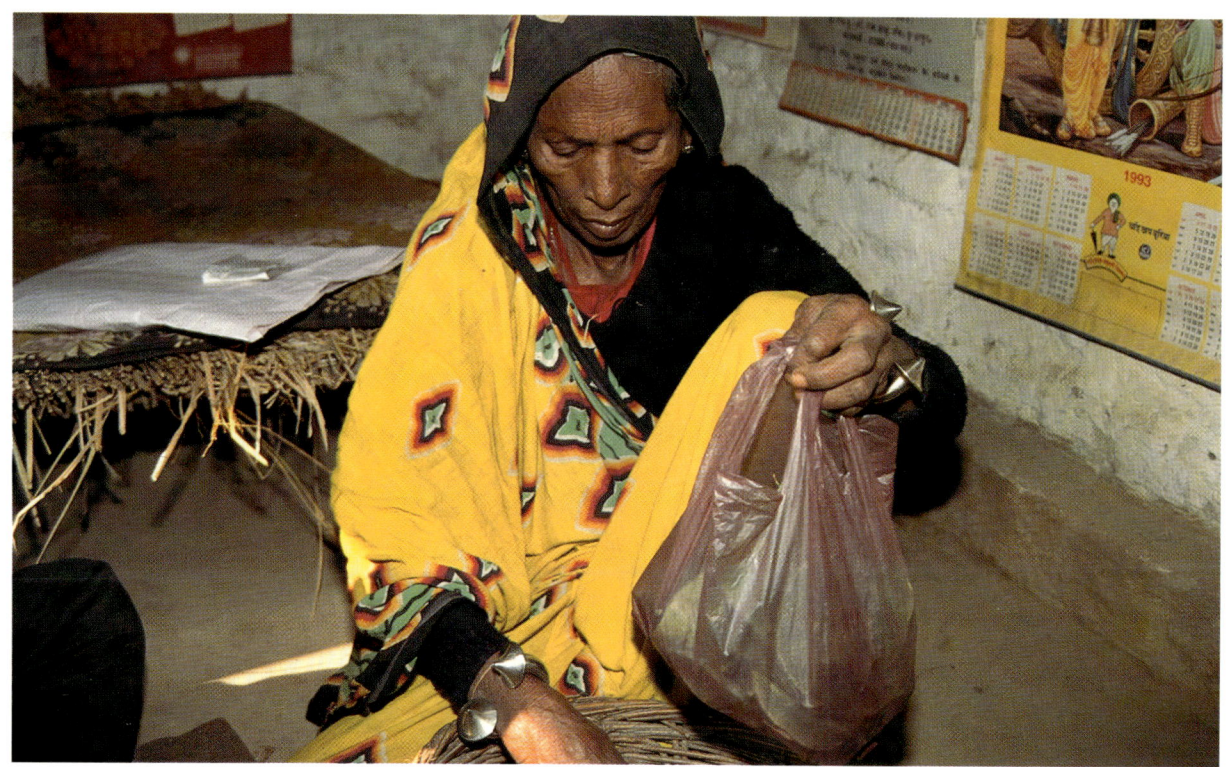

Koshalya in her healing hut.

afford to go to an allopathic doctor in the city of Varanasi, or pay for medicine at pharmacies. Payment to Koshalya, offered privately inside her hut after treatment, usually comes in the form of flowers, food or an offering to the goddess. "My patients have no money for medical doctors in the city, and they don't have faith in that," says Koshalya.

THE HEALING HUT

Koshalya's white healing hut, next to her garden, is sheltered by a thatched roof. Empty clay bowls sit on the well-swept dirt floor. Burlap bags serve as sitting rugs. The room is no larger than ten feet square, and the ceiling in no higher than I am tall: five feet, ten inches. The only piece of furniture in the hut is a straw bed. A concrete ledge, which serves as an altar with candles, fills the wall opposite the entrance. Simple sacred objects of worship, made of clay, plastic, flowers and seeds, decorate the altar.

A second concrete ledge circles the upper part of the hut; it holds dry plants and old jars containing herbs and powders used in healing ceremonies. Pictures of Durga and Siva and water-stained posters of goddesses hang side by side on the mud walls. A damp, earthy odor rises from the floor, while sunlight gleams through holes in the walls.

Twelve village women arrived. One carried a small drum. They gathered under a metal awning protruding from Koshalya's healing hut. The music began. The initial cacophony of strained voices intensified; the drummer found it impossible to keep a beat. The women laughed heartily, arguing at times over the lyrics, but Koshalya always had the final say. Her voice was strong and purposeful.

Eventually the melody, phrasing and lyrics became consonant and mesmerizing. Smiles, body language and drumming suddenly synchronized. Time vanished; the night chilled, but all eyes remained fixed on Koshalya.

She fell into trance. The goddess had "come upon her," and Koshalya was no longer aware of her surroundings. She had opened herself to the effects of the music, something she had obviously and comfortably done many times before.

"I keep myself ready for Sitla through mantra and prayer, and keeping my body clean. Chanting her name and singing attunes me to her essence and vibration," Koshalya later explained.

The women talked gently to their ojha, urging her to return to consciousness and participate in the evening's activities. The verse they had been singing was from the Hindu epic, the "Ramayana." It was a favorite of the goddess Sitla, who had possessed Koshalya, displacing the healer's personality, consciousness and "will" with that of her own. Koshalya slowly regained consciousness and, as if nothing had happened, interacted with her friends.

Since Koshalya's initial experience forty years ago, the goddess of disease regularly enters and leaves Koshalya's mind and body. Once the goddess responds to Koshalya's song by possessing her, other songs and silent mantras are then used to effect cures.

"I have more than twenty-five healing songs; I treat blindness, infertility, jaundice and smallpox and fevers," she said again. "Village babies always have fevers. The music soothes them and lowers body temperature. Sitla is the goddess for cooling the temperature."

SITLA IN AMERICA

"Sitla has called you from America," Koshalya said to me. "I will teach you now. But first you must visit the goddess at her temple." "Can a Western woman do this?" I inquired. "You can use my healing method in your clinic in America, if you have belief in it," the healer answered. She believes Sitla exists in the United States because disease is there. "This is why we must worship her with great respect and offering." Koshalya said. "Without faith in the divine, which has the power to bring disease or take it away, there can be no real protection or healing."

"Sitla is just one name, one aspect of the great Mother goddess who has many manifestations and names in India," Koshalya said. The western world can access healing from the goddess by honoring her through prayer, song and belief. In Christianity, the Holy Spirit, Mother Mary, and female saints could be viewed similarly; in Judaism, the Shechina, or divine feminine side of God, offers another parallel.

Track 2
Koshalya
"Healing Female Reproductive Problems"
This song calls the Goddess Sitla, the goddess of smallpox and disease, "to come upon" Koshalya and alter her state of consciousness in preparation for healing.

The Ganges River and the ancient city of Varanasi

CHAPTER THREE

Ram Tmapa & Suni Ram
Jhankri of Nepal

"The opinion and advice of the Dhamis-Jhankris give balance and direction to the social and religious life of rural Nepal. And since health is so intertwined with religious norms, it is not surprising that Dhamis-Jhankris are seen as the most powerful influences in determining its [health care] course."

*Ramesh M. Shrestha, anthropologist
Institute of Medicine, Nepal*

Faith healing is widely practiced in the mountainous kingdom of Nepal. Nepal is a divergent culture, a blend of many peoples who have passed through or settled in this small country nestled between India and Tibet. From the Tibetan plateau to the north flowed a Mongolian people, who brought their cultures and traditions, including Bon, the pre-Buddhist animist religion. Lowlanders traveling from the southern Gangetic Plain brought with them the Hindu and Buddhist pantheons. All these sacred traditions infuse the daily life of Nepalis, themselves a diverse population of at least a dozen distinct ethnic groups. Nepalese healers have not only coexisted with this variety of traditions but have successfully incorporated elements of the different religions into their practice. In Nepal exists possibly the highest number of healers per capita of any country in the world.

Above: Jhankri Ram Tmapa

"Their function and religion represent a synthesis of the Tibeto-Siberian and Indo-Shamanic traditions, apparently deriving much of the symbolism and mythology from Tibeto-Siberian culture, with a Hindu orientation and many Hindu features."

Casper J. Miller, anthropologist

Nepalese healers are called *Dhamis-Jankris* or simply *Jhankris*. They practice "folk psychiatry" to reduce culture-specific stress, anxiety and other psychological disorders. Healing rituals *(cinta)* harness and incorporate the psychic energy, social history and mythology of the patient and community in an effort to heal. Thus jhankris serve as therapeutic and religious leaders of paramount importance to the Nepalese people in rural areas.

> "In the Nepalese belief system, [which] has existed for generations and is linked to deep-rooted religious precepts, illness is often associated with spirit possession: therefore, the appropriate healer is the faith healer, who is perceived as a skilled medium capable of placating hostile invading spirits.
>
> *Dr. Mahendra Chhetri*
> *Regional Medical Officer, Nepal*

In 1980, fewer than 500 medical doctors were in Nepal's government services. Even though this number has increased somewhat, most physicians do not serve in the rural areas where ninety-five percent of Nepalis live. Thus, there are between 400,000 and 800,000 faith healers in rural Nepal. The jhankri is both a priest and physician. He or she is not regarded as a threat by priests of established religions but instead fills a needed function outside organized faith. The jhankri is versed in preventative care and curative health rituals for human beings and animals.

Rural Nepalese seek the help of a jhankri to treat physical illness or solving economic woes, like crop failure. Problems with marriage and other relationships are also part of the jhankri's therapeutic domain. In a country as impoverished as Nepal, faith healers often offer the only health care and counseling to rural villagers. The jhankri is also popular in the cities, as Western medicine does not yet offer help with personal problems, which remains the province of the jhankri. Members of high and low castes use their services. Fees are adjusted on a sliding scale, from a small bag of rice to whole goats and water buffaloes. Rural jhankri seldom rely on the healing arts to make a living. They also farm, herd livestock and practices various trades.

A patient comes to a jhankri to receive a cinta. The healer uses mantras and magical verses, given him by a guru or deity. Most jhankri have received instruction from a teacher who excels in a particular area of cures, such as overthrowing the powers of misfortune or specific diseases. Some begin their training as children, taught in caves or in the home of a guru. Jhankris who have studied with one or several skilled teachers enjoy distinction. On the other hand, a self-proclaimed jhankri practices under the direct guidance of a deity. The calling comes in dreams or through an experience of possession. Shaking is a sign of being touched by a god and is part of the jhankri experience. Age is not important, only skill and results.

> *"By incorporating a mantra's magic within his heart, throat and limbs, a melody echoing others through its sinewy folds and assonant rhymes, an apprentice healer begins to incarnate a sensibility that goes beyond the linguistic."*
>
> Robert R. Desjarlais,
> Anthropologist

The jhankri's primary musical instrument is a large two-headed drum, the *dhyangro*. It is played with *agajo*, a long snake-shaped drumstick made from cane. The wooden drum frames are covered with the skins of mountain goats. Straw talismans, old coins and other good-luck pieces may be concealed inside the drum. You can hear them when the drums are struck or shaken.

For the Nepalese, there is no separation between the jhankri and the dhyangro. To own and hold the drum signifies wisdom earned and understood by true healers. Some faith healers discard

Jhankri Ram Tmapa in trance.

their drums when the deity that possesses them does not respond favorably to its sound. In this case, the jhankri will use a metal pan and strike it with his traditional gajo. Always, a large garland of bells hangs around the healer's neck or is worn as a belt.

When beating the drum, the jhankri often performs a circular two-stepped hopping dance. The rhythm of the drum and the simple dance synchronize and create a more kinesthetic than cerebral experience for both patient and healer, who both transition into another state of consciousness through the sound. The patient must be induced to return swiftly to the body, instead of continuing to disassociate or separate from the present world, allowing disease to ensue. When the jhankri is not dancing he sits cross-legged on the floor, beating the drum and reciting sacred mantras. He waits for the arrival of his aiding deity. When the god comes the jhankri "shakes." He blurts out the cause and treatment for an illness.

CINTA

Ram Chandra Tmapa, a twenty-two year-old jhankri, performs healing rituals only when someone is ill. He does not predict the future or solve marital problems. A Nepalese man named Raj approached Ram to request a cinta for his aged mother, who is dying. Raj's mother has been ill for years, confined to a bed in a small room inside his house. Twelve people crowd into the sick woman's room, including her grandchildren, children, some of Raj's workers and local village friends.

Before the healing takes place, Ram organizes a small work area and dons necklaces of bells. He sits cross-legged in the middle of the floor and withdraws into himself. The jhankri's assistant blesses the money offered on a plate of rice with incense and prayer. Ram then closes his eyes and begins drumming — pounding on a large, stainless steel pie plate offered by the ill woman's daughter-in-law. The jhankri brought his own agajo, with metal bands of embossed designs and metal tip. Relatives and friends chatter loudly over the din until the timbre and quality of the jhankri's voice changes in timbre and quality. When the gods come to speak through the jhankri, everyone quiets. Ram's body begins to vibrate intensely and the clanging pie tin drops away, replaced by violent shaking and vocalizing. The ringing, clanging garlands of bells mimic the rhythm of the shaking body. The jhankri's head thrashes back and forth, his vibrating lips flap and his sunken eyes remain closed. Then begin the unworldly utterances, one word at a time.

He stops to take a breath. He removes the bells, suggesting that the god-spirit is at hand and will come quickly when the drumming resumes. In the session that follows, the plate-banging is brief and Ram soon starts shaking uncontrollably. His eyes sometimes open. The soft spoken jhankri succumbs to the personality of the spirit speaking through him.

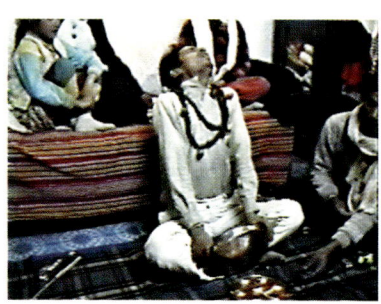

Dhyangro, a jhankri drum.

SUNI RAM

Suni Ram, seventy-one years old in this photo, lives in a high mountain village in the Annapurna range. He learned his art from his father and is now teaching his son. He specializes in curing physical illness caused by black magic. In one case, an American traveller has been suffering from severe stomach pains. The jhankris's wife invited the patient to sit by the fire pit in the center of their one-room home. Suni Ram took the wrists of the patient to help him diagnose her problem, and unhooked his drum from the wall and began to beat it. He danced around the fire and chanted sacred mantra. He put down his drum and knelt beside the woman, bowing his head and placing his face near her stomach.

"Possessed, he laughs and demands beer, and when someone brings him a stainless steel cup full, he gulps a swig. The assistant who accompanies Ram asks questions about the woman's illness. Ram fires responses. The speaking spirit tone is assertive, direct and authoritative. At times, it also jokes, making everyone laugh. Someone then lifts the sick old woman out of her bed and moves her closer to the healer. Her bone-thin legs crossed, her back in a dejected hunch, she looks at the jhankri with the look of one too tired with life to hide her feelings anymore, who's seen all and has no hope, and yet a sparkle in the eye toward the jhankri reveals that she still has faith."

Tamia Marg Anderson
Observer

"Without even touching his lips to my skin, he appears to be extracting something from my body. He spits out what looks to be coagulated blood. The jhankri warns me about some people practicing black magic against me. And some food that I ate was bad, he tells me. He treats a piece of flat roasted bread right off the fire with my Swiss army knife — to make it safe for me to eat. Then he makes blessings on packages of uncooked colored rice, a few grains each for everyone in our group to take on on journey."

Tamia Marg Anderson
Observer

Once the jhankri delivered his instruction — to bathe the sick woman in hot water, over her whole body — the family put the old woman to bed. Both the woman and her family reflected renewed energy. Questioned after the session, Ram claimed he could not remember anything. He explained that when the god speaks through him he is not himself. "I have been healing others since I was fifteen years old. I had three years of training and four years of practice. I am also self-taught. The gods first called me through my dreams!"

Track 3
Ram Tmapa and Suni Ram
"Giving Energy to a Dying Woman"
"Healing a Woman with Stomach Pain"
Two Nepalese Jhankris perform healing rituals: Ram Tmapa self-induces a trance state by clanging a brass cooking plate and performing intense vocalizations. The energy from his sound transfers to a dying woman bringing life back into her body. Suni Ram beats the traditional jhankri drum dhyangro until a diagnosis is confirmed. He places his mouth to the patient's stomach and extracts foreign objects held there that are causing the pain. She is healed in the process.

Suni Ram and his wife outside their Himalayan village home.

Don Agustin Rivas-Vasquez
Peruvian Ayahuasca Shaman

"Every night I sang the icaros and mariris that came to me. The icaros came first; they are tunes without words. Then I would add mariris, the words, according to which plant I was drinking."

Don Agustin

Don Agustin Rivas-Vasquez is a healer in the Amazon jungle. His medicine of choice comes from "Mother Ayahuasca," a vine that natives have used for thousands of years. He performs "surgical operations," and he leads group healings with song, harmonica and rattles to help cleanse the body of sickness.

Don Agustin was born in a town called Tamshiyacu, three hours by boat south of Iquitos, in eastern Peru. He spent much of his childhood investigating nature along the Amazon river and was a folk sculptor until an accident damaged the nerves in his arms and hands. He still carves and sculpts, but is now a dedicated full-time healer.

This shaman began his training twenty-seven years ago under several native healers. Don Agustin's training included fasting, abstaining from sex with his wife for extended periods of time and living in a hollowed-out tree. His personal sacrifice took six years. Don Agustin said, "You have to have love for this kind of work and for the medicines."

It was clear that to heal more serious illnesses, such as cancer, the Ayahuascero must be skilled in communicating with spirits. He must be able to call on them for help in a healing session. "It is the spirits that do the healing, I am simply a middleman," said Don Agustin.

He learned his songs from his native teachers and from the Mother Plant, as well as spirits who aid in healings, he continued. "All of my music is called shamanic music. All of the ceremonial songs are sung in Quechua."

He returned to his home town several years ago and built an encampment called Yushintaita, two hours' hike into the jungle. Among his people, he is known as an *Ayahuascero,* an Ayahuasca shaman.

"Here in the jungle I have 600 hectares of land, where we help people from all over the world who are suffering from sicknesses that medical science is still unable to cure. Here, we are creating ways of curing. We are trying to cure some cancer cases and some cases of illness with unknown causes," said Don Agustin.

His *icaros* and *mariris* are used for learning and healing. "Ayahuasca was my primary teacher," says Don Agustin. The Mother Plant revealed to him, in visions, which medicinal plants to investigate.

Above: Don Agustin Rivas-Vasquez

Spirits often came in human form to teach the icaros, or tunes, of different trees and plants. "These are part of my jungle studies," said Don Agustin.

As an accomplished musician and student of Quechua, the ancient Inca language, he incorporated Quechua words into the icaros. "That's how I learned the Quechua mariris that I use for curing and working with Ayahuasca," said the shaman.

These extraordinary songs help people who have trouble sleeping, and can be played during massage. These songs are used to work on human sensitivities, and can cause listeners to vomit, cry, scream and experience any other mental or bodily effect that deals with placement, beliefs and life experience. Don Agustin said, "When you have these reactions, healing is taking place. The body holds many oxidations, toxins and phlegm. They can be expelled through my work."

First, Faith in God

These songs and the Ayahuasca vine are the only things that can help heal human beings at the deepest levels. Also, if a person does not believe in anything, then that person cannot believe in God, said Don Agustin. "We must believe! My work includes God, therefore, if a hand is laid upon someone [a patient], it is the hand of God that is guiding me."

"The cries are very important because they help rid you of things that have been buried there for many years, from tragedies," said Don Agustin. "This is done in the form of tears. The songs and the plant medicine penetrate the stomach and cause vomiting — the more vomiting the better. This means it will be a good healing ceremony. Vomiting opens up the internal tract, allowing it to release toxins and oxidants that have been held for many, many years. It rids the body of them. They all disappear."

Surgical Operations

The Ayahuasca shaman performs non-invasive "surgical operations" with rattles and ceremonial rods. He can treat several patients in a single session. "I can operate on a person's body and cut the illness out with my mind," he says. "I start at 9 o'clock in the evening and then at 2 o'clock, the operations take place." The rods are used to point, mocking surgical knives ready to cut away maladies. When the patient is "cut," in the imagination of the healer, a type of scratching, probing or pulling-out of the infirmities takes place. "Then the sickness can come out when we use our imaginations well," says the healer.

Don Agustin with Ayahuasca pipe.

Don Agustin harvesting plants in the Peruvian jungle.

Don Agustin shared a story: "A young man with tumors in his head came to see me. The doctors wanted to open him up, and I told him I could help him. He had prepared himself with great faith. During the first night, I took the tumors out of his head. You could see the tumors outside of his head. They were small. After that I didn't feel any problem. He called his mom, and she invited me to [visit her in] Spain for a week. She told the Spaniards that I had cured her son."

The healer must close his eyes and rest for a few moments before the next stage of work. During this silence, Don Agustin's aides deliver invocations and prayers so that the healings (operations) can take effect. The rattles keep the tempo for the songs, the icaros and the whistling. The precious metals inside the rattles, gyrating and spiraling up and down, play an important role, as they are thought to pull the sickness out of the patient.

Mother Ayahuasca

"During the Ayahuasca ceremony, we invoke the healing of the world," Don Agustin says. "We learn from Mother Ayahuasca that we must respect the earth so that we can continue to live on it. That is why we vomit, moan and cry."

Icaros enrich the Ayahuasca experience. Ayahuasca is a plant that has been used for healing in the Amazon for millenia. "Before we had hospitals, clinics, and doctors, we used Ayahuasca to cure our people. Even today people still come in search of a shaman to cure them," said Don Agustin.

Songs of the Ayahuasca Ceremony

There is a specific order to the songs and their purpose in the Ayahuasca ceremony. After an introductory invocation, mariris and icaros start the ceremony. These healing words can be sung or blown through the breath into a harmonica or smoke and are referred to as "blows." The blows open the body conduits.

In the introduction to the ceremony, a blessing is sung, called "Caypin Llapanchis Cachicanicua." This mariri is sung in adoration and honors Mother Ayahuasca. Following this song, an invocation is sung to honor all the great healers that are still alive or have passed on.

Don Agustin playing the antara (pan pipe).

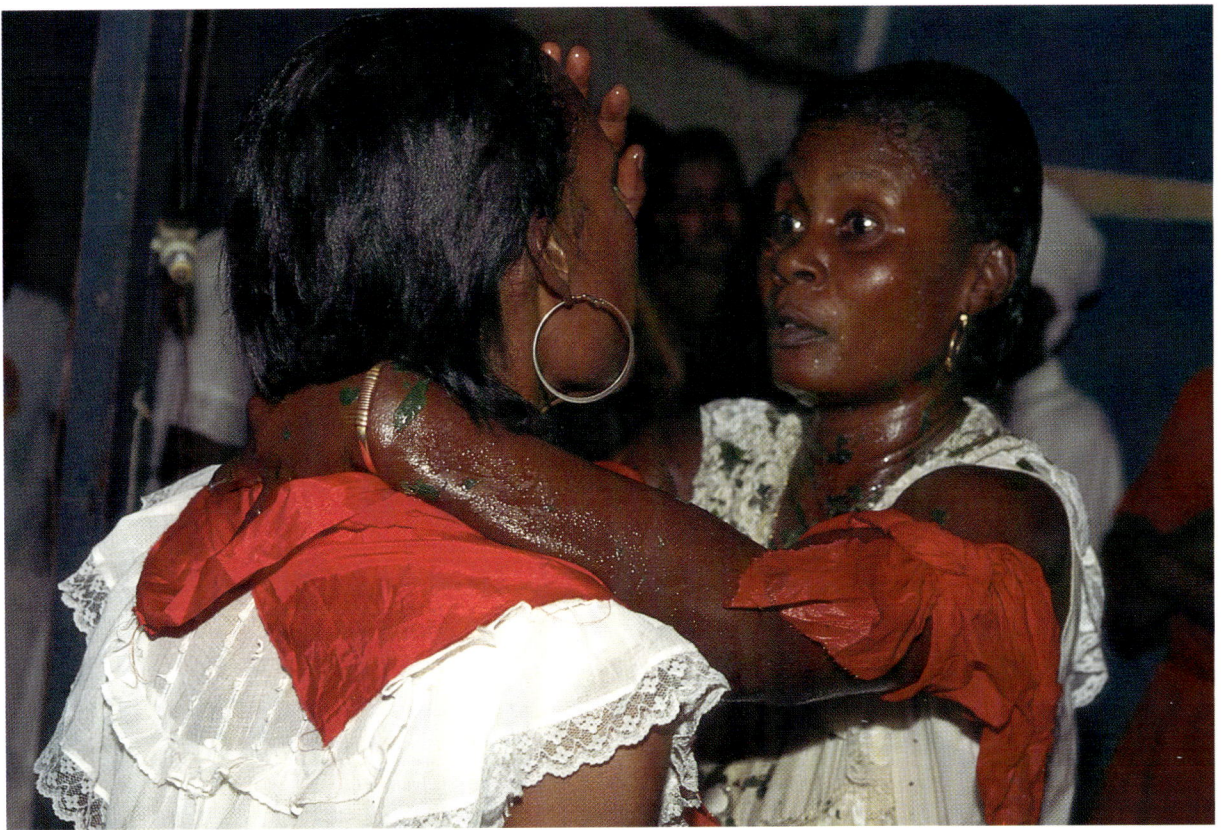

Ezili Dantò, the feminine divinity of motherhood, magic and healing, performs a healing blessing for a woman suffering an illness in a Vodou society.

To use leaves in a remedy, "you can [brew] tea or [use them] in a bath. You bathe the person. You rub the leaves all over their body to take out what's bad. We use all kinds of leaves. You take it and make a pomade with out of it. You crush it, mix it with medicines, and put it on the body to reduce swelling." She added, "You might boil it up and have the person eat it, or fry it in oil. You put somebody back the way they were, and then you send them home."

The power of leaves comes from Gran Mèt, who blesses them, from our guardian angels, and from the *mystè* (spirits). God is in front, and the angels are behind. When the angel gets good enough, God gives it the power to heal.

When asked what causes people to seek her out, Forestal replied, "A lot of people come to me for treatment; there are always people here. It's like a little hospital. I see all kinds of sickness. Some have high fevers, diarrhea, vomiting. Here we give remedies to take down the vomiting or the diarrhea. We chase away the bad spirits. But if there were no bad spirits on the person, we send them to the doctor. That's a case for a doctor."

Music is essential to the manbo's art, as Forestal explained: "Drums are freedom. When the drum beats, it gives you strength. Then we have power. If we were weak, we would call *Papa Feray* and *Gran Ezili* (Afro-Haitian deities), and while we were calling them they would give us strength. Then we don't feel weak anymore. Then the spirits might come and do a treatment — and they do it right. And if the treatment doesn't work, the spirit will have already seen that, it's because the person sank too low. The spirit can't do anything for them."

Written by Elizabeth McAlister Ph.D.

Track 5
Micheline Forestal
"Healing with Leaves Ceremony"
The music offered here was recorded at a spiritual familial compound called the Lakou Badjo, near Gonaives, Haiti, in July of 1996. The song says "Ou a pile fey-mwen," ("You are crushing my leaves"), and is played to the rhythm called Kongo, from the rite (series of rituals) of the same name.

CHAPTER SIX

Kanucas Littlefish
Native American Anishnabe Medicine Man

"Great Spirit" take pity on my relatives

Kishi Manitou manshuwan indouwhen

Muquay Manitou manshuwan inniniiquey ininiimish

Bear Spirit take pity on these good women, these good men.

Kanucas Littlefish
Song to Heal the Body and Spirit

The jagged glacier-clad mountains of the Olympic Range surge abruptly from the land mass of the Olympic Peninsula, in the extreme northwest corner of the contiguous United States. The winters here are long and wet and the mountains are often shrouded by thick clouds that sweep in from the Pacific. The land is verdant despite years of logging and thick evergreen forests flourish everywhere.

Ice-age glaciers carved up the land and then retreated, leaving a vast network of waterways. Kanucas Littlefish and his family live on the edge of the peninsula overlooking the Hood Canal, one of these many meandering expanses of water.

Two hawthorn trees, their boughs heavy with deep pink blossoms, stand beside the path to their home. There is a sweat lodge on the little hill out back. Kanukus, his wife Nancy, and their daughter Mashkiki live here, and there are always people visiting. Sometimes they come for a sweat and a meal, sometimes for a few months or longer.

"We're a safe house for red road refugees (Native Americans)," Nancy says with good humor. She serves as a bridge, a counselor and friend to those who come here looking for something real, a spiritual connection that is strong and vital. Many are Native Americans, others are Asian, black or white. People of all races are welcome.

Kanacus Littlefish is many things. He is a spiritual leader, a healer, a sun dancer, a father, uncle, brother and friend to many. Most people simply call him Ken.

"I am an Anishnabe (Chippewa) Indian," Ken said, "of the Ottertail Pilligar band of the Turtle Clan. I was born on the 12th day of the fourth month of the 1,946th year, to Robert Leonard Durant, an Ottowa, and Maxine Stanley, an Ojibbewa. I was born dead in Chicago Cook County hospital, state of Illinois. I am a 'veil baby.' The spirit brought me back to life on that morning of April 12th. I have died three more times since, and the spirit has sent me back. The fifth time I was dying with a bone disease that went into remission."

"The women on my mother's side have all been in a 'medicine way' as far back as eight generations. I am the first male in my family to pick up the medicine since then." Ken explained that the

Above: Kanucas Littlefish

women in his family practiced their skills quietly, skills that involved a deep understanding of the use of herbs, roots, and flowers.

When Ken was born his grandmother knew his path was to be the medicine way. At six months, Ken was diagnosed with polio which left him with a crippling scoliosis. These illnesses have left their mark, and Ken is no stranger to physical challenges. His family went through difficult times and he was placed in several foster homes where he was severely mistreated. At the age of five, Ken was sent to a reformatory, a Catholic boarding school for "incorrigible children," where he lived until he was eighteen.

During this time, his innate power as a healer began to reveal itself. Other children came to him when they were sick or hurt. He cared for them, they got well, and he became known as "Doc." The years of his youth were hard, and he was completely isolated from the traditions of his people.

At nineteen, Ken was challenged further by the loss of his left hand in an industrial accident. It was shortly after this that he attended his first tepee meeting (Native American Church meeting). It was the beginning of the road back to the medicine way — back to what he was born to do.

"As a veil baby," Ken said, "according to our people, I could have picked up anything I wanted to do. I don't know how the spirit moves people to do what they do. It was on a vision quest that it showed me how it wanted it to be with me. That's when I started doing what I'm doing. Among other things, I was told to work with all the races, not just the Indian people."

People come to Ken for all reasons; for problems with health, addictions and relationships. Some people come wanting a ceremony to give thanks. Ken feels very strongly about alcohol and drug abuse. As a healer and man he is compassionate but firm about his position, and will help people if they are first willing to help themselves.

Ken knows many songs and uses them in healing. "Some time back," Ken explained, "a man I hardly knew then came into a sweat [lodge] where I was pouring water. He was deaf in one ear. I began singing and when I was done he had his hearing back. Another time a man had a broken leg when he came into the sweat lodge. When he left he was able to walk upon that leg without pain or a limp."

"When I sing I use vocables and words in my native language. Lines of power exist all around us. What I try to do is tap into that power through sound and vibration using my voice and a drum. I also use a rattle, a gourd or a deer-horn shaker. When the lines of power are met, it is said a healing can occur."

Ken says, "All of life is a ceremony, a life prayer. This life prayer takes place every day in how you think, how you talk and how you act. Whatever takes place, whatever format or ceremony we use, what I am seeing is that real love is capable of bringing up the spirit. Certain formats, such as ceremonies, prayers and songs are what they call traditions."

"Today, some people are touched by the spirit, people who don't have traditional ways but who have a real love for all of life, all forms of life. So this unconditional love is more prevalent today at a time when it is really necessary."

"But unconditional love also takes a commitment, a discipline as strong as any tradition. It takes a commitment to the spirit's unconditional love, to purity of spirit, purity of mind, purity of heart and purity of the body, with eternal faith in the spirit. I sing to heal the spirit and the body. They are inseparable."

Written by Pat Moffitt Cook & Susan Elaine Brown

Track 6 Kanacus Littlefish "Curing Serious Illness" Kanacus Littlefish sings this song to heal serious illnesses. The spirit and energy of the sound intercepts the course of illness.

Kanacus Littlefish playing a drum.

CHAPTER SEVEN

Maestro Demosdenes Ramirez Hurtas

Kuna Indian Song Healer of the San Blas Islands

"I always go to my patient's house at four, five or six o'clock. This is the best time to catch the devil; because he is active at night! After food offerings are laid out for the *nuchus* [medicine dolls], I lay down in a hammock near my patient. I begin to concentrate. In my head there is a cassette tape…it remembers the entire "Nia Ikar" [song for mental illness] which will play non-stop for four days. I allow the song to become all there is, taking me over. It is dangerous to fight the *Nia* [devil], so in the first part of my song I remember my ancestors and my power. When I am ready for battle…I go on to the next part."

Maestro Demosdenes Ramirez Hurtas

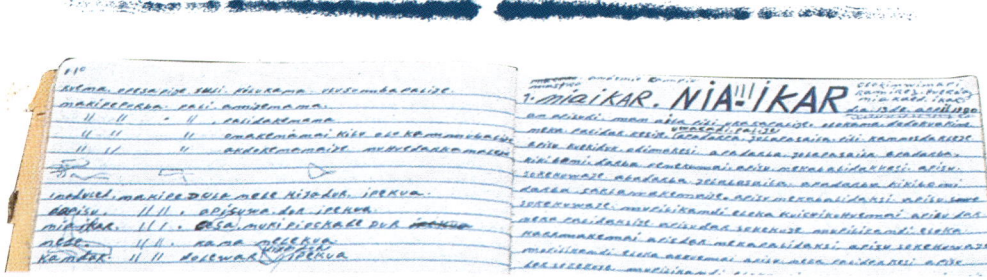

Above: Maestro singing the Nia Ikar, the song for mental illness.
Bottom: Pages of the Nia Ikar from the Maestro's handwritten songbook.

Song healer Maestro Demosdenes Ramirez suffers from cataracts in both eyes. "I have almost passed sixty years and can't read my handwriting any more. I hope to go to Panama City for eye surgery. The government will pay for the surgery, but I have no money for airfare."

He buried his head in his song book and continued interpreting the "Nia Ikar." He wiped his brow. The heat was getting to all of us.

Here I am seated on this stool, high on the mountain top as is our custom.
From here I can see the oceans, mountains, and rivers and feel the sun, wind and rain
Like these elements
I am powerful
Like the North and South winds coming together to fight
I must come together with the devil for battle
I concentrate all of my energy and power
I sit here on this stool like my ancestors,
high on the mountain top
as is our custom…
gathering my power.

The Opening of the "Nia Ikar"
Song for Mental illness

"My book contains songs my maestro taught me. His name is Otis and he has passed ninety years now," Demosdenes explained. "I have another maestro who has passed one hundred years, but can't walk. Their medicine song books are made of pictures, not words, like mine. I remember the days when they 'sang the pictures.' Now no one, except my teachers and the néles, can understand the hieroglyphics and drawings anymore."

Demosdenes pointed to the second verse and said, "These words cannot be spoken. You must sing them. It's impossible to translate shamanic language exactly, even into Kuna. I can only create a picture in your mind and give you the idea of the words!" He shook his head and remembered when he began learning the "Nia Ikar," back in 1972.

"It took three years to "embody" this song in my nerves, brain and heart," he said. "The words are easy, but to experience the song's power, and use it for healing, takes three years." Demosdenes recounted what Otis said to him.

"First you must learn other medicine songs to build strength inside. Later I will teach you the "Song of Mental Illness." If you are not prepared, this song will harm you. Your own mind will become unstable. The very center of you will get confused. Some students become physically and mentally ill. Too many nightmares and frightening visions come."

Each maestro specializes in several treatments. Among these are songs for alcoholism, infertility and severe headache. Maestro Ramirez is best known for curing those people suffering from mental illness and for helping the dead journey to paradise. "I excel in two areas; the "Masar" (the "Song of the Dead") and "Nia Ikar." I take herbs and liquids to soothe my throat and keep it open."

When a Kuna Indian dies, the soul travels upward toward paradise. The soul has no voice and must encounter one hundred *sailas* (chiefs) on one hundred islands along its journey. The maestro is the spokesperson for the travelling soul. He sings the Masar, which negotiates safe and respectful passage from each island chief. It takes two days to complete this process and is sung sitting up.

Maestro Demosdenes telling healing stories.

In any treatment, if the maestro fails to cure his patient he must perform the song in its entirety again. In the "Nia Ikar," the nuchus and ancestors play central roles. They battle the devil on behalf of the patient. The song itself creates a "living dramatic stage." The maestro's voice, fueled by shamanic words, creates a stimulating aural fabric that mesmerizes and carries the patient to another reality where the battle with mental illness can be won. The maestro himself shows no emotion or response to the story or imagery. He simply sings the story without emphasis or dynamics. He sways in a hammock, and his voice sounds as if it rises up from another realm.

The Song for Mental Illness

"When the world was created there was nothing in it. The first thing that appeared were trees, thirty different kinds. The wood of the different trees carry (house) the original spirit of the nuchus," said Demosdenes. Out of these various woods nuchus are carved in the image of ancestors, great sailas, powerful néles and international superheros. Each family has a box of nuchus to call on in times of crisis or illness.

The Kuna Indians believe that mental illness and paranoia are caused by the devil disturbing the mind. "There are devils from the sea, jungle, sky and four directions but the devil from the north *(Nia Galu)* is the most powerful and destructive," said the maestro. "Its power is like a tornado or hurricane." To capture a devil, the maestro sings the "Nia Ikar," which doesn't call the devil directly but instead entices him to come and check on the person he is tormenting. It is performed in three parts, each part preparing the nuchus, spirits and patient for the devil's capture.

Three nuchus are called to fight. Once the battle begins, the devil changes form rapidly. This is meant to confuse eight helping spirits (male and female) and the nuchus. The devil must go through thirty-seven transformations before he can be captured. Before the nuchus take on the devil in his final form they all change their clothes. "They dress formally to show how strong they are. It is not good to just be in everyday clothes," said the maestro. In ancient times, their clothing was changed entirely; today, only their blouses and shirts are replaced.

Now formally dressed, the nuchus and eight spirits cast a magic net over the devil. Once caught in the net, the devil struggles wildly. "Sometimes the patient gets more sick here," said the maestro. "But when the nuchus finally take the devil to the lowest level of the underworld, the patient begins to heal. They burn the devil first and then bury him forever. The devil from the North is taken to his city in the north and burned."

The Future

"These ways will be finished by the year 2000," predicts the maestro. "Already, there is no one who can sing the pictures. I had two students for a while but they do not come often. To be a maestro takes time and patience. They are more interested in travelling to the mainland and finding work. I know the songs will disappear. That is why I am willing to sing for you."

Track 7
Maestro Demosdenes Ramirez Hurtas
"Healing Mental Illness"
Maestro sings the opening of the "Nia Ikar" (the way of mental illness). Recorded in the San Blas Islands in June 1996.

Maestro and Pat Moffitt Cook walking in Ustupu discussing Kuna healng methods. His staff symbolizes political status and power. A nuchu doll is carved on the top.

CHAPTER EIGHT

Darikiking Don Alejandro
Amazon Medicine Man

"I know when people hear my ancestors' healing songs they awaken and feel a new thirst for life. It's not important to know my dialect because . . . it is in the rhythm . . . the melody . . . the sounds of the rain forest. This desire to live brings us back into balance."

— Darikiking

"Neither his ancestors nor he himself knew who had taught them their ancient songs. They simply felt that with these melodies they could meditate, heal and connect with nature and the powerful voice of the Amazon," said the healer's student, Richard Aguayo.

Darikiking doesn't know his date of birth; such details get lost in the time and space of the primordial Amazonian jungle of southeastern Peru. "I believe it was sometime in the 1940s," he says. "Darikiking is my natural name. It connects me to nature and fills me with joy. My name is the sound the rain forest makes when day is giving way to night."

Darikiking Alejandro Jahuanchi, his full name, lives in the Cuzco and Madre de Dios region of the Peruvian Amazon rain forest. Don Alejandro was the name he was given when his community came into contact with Catholic missionaries. They called him Don Alejandro, as a sign of respect and recognition of his great wisdom and his love of the forest.

When asked about his parents, Darikiking shared vivid memories of his mother, who was in contact with the jaguar. "The jaguar is a powerful animal who helps protect and heal us. This spirit protected her at all times," he said.

"My father made contact with the spirits of the rain forest. Forest spirits carried my father off when he was a young boy, and made known to him the natural world," Darikiking remembered. The spirits taught him specific healing rituals and songs. They revealed to him that plants and trees are "beings" like ourselves, but "we can only communicate with them when we are in a state of ecstasy, meditation or when we are truly innocent," he said. These things still happened, only…maybe…sixty years ago."

The healer doesn't offer many clues about his present-day life. Instead, he delivers a message, a hope that somewhere inside ourselves we connect deeper and experience a forgotten but essential spiritual wisdom. "We have become too concerned with material and social things," he says. "This has clouded our sacred memories — distracting us from the knowledge of good health, balance and a respectful relationship with nature."

Above: Darikiking Don Alejandro

Opposite page: Darikiking praying to his ancestors.

"His ethnic community, the Huachipayri [also known as Wa-chi-pie], are accustomed to living without any markers for the passing of time, simply knowing that nature is perennial," says Aguayo.

The Huachipayri People

The Huachipayri tribe escaped Incan conquest several hundred years before the Europeans arrived. The Amazon jungle terrain made warfare difficult and protected the tribes that sought its refuge. Because of this, many Indians in the deep Amazon remained true to their original culture.

In the 16th century, the Huachipayri were among those Peruvian indigenous groups gravely affected by the arrival of foreign explorers and colonists. Retreating this time to the most remote part of the jungle, they hid for generations. No fires were made or jungle trails cut for fear of being discovered and mistreated. Ritual practices and native customs thus survived untainted. The jungle sustained the Huachipayri physically and spiritually until the present century.

Darikiking praying to his ancestors.

THE TREE OF LIFE

"LONG AGO, WHEN THE WORLD WAS IN GREAT DANGER FROM DROUGHT AND FIRE, A TREE SPRANG FORTH FROM THE LOINS OF A WOMAN OF GREAT PURITY. ALL THE ANIMALS AND HUMAN BEINGS CLIMBED INTO ITS BRANCHES AND SAVED THEMSELVES FROM DESTRUCTION. THIS TREE WAS CALLED THE HUANAYMEY TREE."

Darikiking praying to the spirit of the Jaguar.

The Huachipayri people speak their own native language. Spanish is spoken more frequently today as they become more influenced by Peruvian and Spanish culture.

THE SEVENTH GENERATION

According to Huachipayri prophecies, in every seventh generation a master leader or teacher is born. One of the best known among them was Ijpeng, "Brother to the Wind." He could manifest and demanifest his physical form at will. The "Mystery" gave him great powers as a spiritual warrior. After Ijpeng came the others: Anancyhua, Chinion, Chicon, Huascren, Sanenura and finally Darikiking, thus fulfilling the prophecy of the appearance of a great master every seven generations.

Darikiking, upon assuming the leadership of his tribe, led his people back to their homelands, which they had fled decades earlier. During this difficult and painful period, he began to teach the ancient traditions he had inherited. He began to reorganize his community, to recover many of the ceremonies which had been lost and to serve as a healer. He is greatly esteemed by his people and by outsiders.

Despite his efforts, many of his people were losing their traditions. Thus he renounced his leadership and began wandering alone in the forest, searching for the special place he saw in his ceremonies with the Mother Plant. Once he found it, he built a center for students and patients called *Huanaymey*, The Tree of Life, and the Center for Traditional Medicine, near Pilcopata, in the province of Kosnipata, in southeastern Peru.

Don Alejandro told the story of Huanaymey: "Long ago, when the world was in great danger from drought and fire, a tree sprang forth from the loins of a woman of great purity. All the animals and human beings climbed into its branches and saved themselves from destruction. This tree was called the Huanaymey tree."

Don Alejandro named his center for this legendary tree, symbolizing hope for the preservation of an endangered philosophy, its traditions and its ceremonies. "The rituals and songs must be saved and practiced for the well being of others . . . for their healing," said Don Alejandro. Since the center opened in 1990, people from all over the world have come to visit and learn.

"His family heritage and legacy cultivated within him traditional wisdom and abilities to communicate with the "Mystery." He is the seventh in a line of warriors, leaders and healers. He remains closely connected to past spiritual leaders, who often appear before him when he conducts his ceremonies with the Mother Plant," says Richard Aguayo.

"Mother Plant"

Darikiking communicates in deep meditation with diseased masters of his tribe, such as Daripikumpa, who discovered and made the very first contact with the "Mother Plant," or Camarambi, six years years ago. Previous masters who discovered other plants called them "Elementals." These are still used in ceremonies, for explorations, in healings, or for clairvoyance and for sensing danger. "Coca leaves can be used to tell the future," he said.

Don Alejandro was taught how to use all of these plants but said, "I feel most connected to Ayahuasca." He uses it together with breath and song during healings and sacred ceremony. Because of this he calls it the "Mother Plant," the "Elemental Plant" or the "Mystery Plant." "When someone who is sick touches the great mystery, healing can occur."

In preparation for healing sessions, Darikiking Don Alejandro performs the ritual of approaching, cutting and gathering the Mother Plant; the ritual of crushing the Mother Plant and the ritual of preparing the Mother Plant. The sound of chopping and breaths and singing accompany the ritual and preparations of the Mother Plant.

Touching the Mystery

The healer's songs touch the Mystery. "The Mystery is the superior power, the creator and constant in life," says Darikiking. "Songs and rituals strike an echo within us . . . This same echo will resonate with the natural elements in the place where we are listening. People will feel the sweetness of life flowering inside of them, as they heal."

Since 1994, Don Alejandro has begun sharing his knowledge in Europe and the United States. Conferences have been held in universities, medical centers, schools and at the White House in Washington, DC.

During one conference he commented, "The world has changed so much because humans have become distanced from their own body and spirit. They have lost their self-esteem, self-education and self-equilibrium in nutrition. Which is to say they have lost their love, will and hope, through feeling self-sufficient on the material plane and not believing in the Mystery, in the invisible we call spirit. It is part of the Mystery."

"If someone is sick with headaches and stress we must call and sing for the wild turkey. He can untangle the knots within ourselves. This illness happens because we rush to acquire material things, which disturbs both our spirit and our nervous system. I sing and wait for the wild turkey to come."

"If we have a very strong impression or a psychic shock our astral body will leave us abruptly. We must call it back with rituals so that it can return without negative consequences with the ritual of calling the lost spirits," he said.

"I sing for you here the ritual for healing intestinal colics," he offered. "When we have no discipline in our personal diet our physical body does not function properly. We must improve our diet and perform this ritual, calling the spirit of the jaguar," said Darikiking, as he prepared to sing.

Track 8
Darikiking
"Ritual for Healing Digestive Disorders"
Often our psychological ills affect our internal systems, such as the digestive system. When we call the spirit of the agouti it will help us to correct this imbalance. An agouti is a rodent related to guinea pigs found in Latin America. It was performed in 1996 by Darikiking at Huanaymey, his healing clinic in the Amazon Jungle.

CHAPTER NINE

Alexander Tavakay
Tuvan Shaman

"In a perfectly performed ritual the drumming is good, and the shaman's soul will go out of his body. It will fly high over the mountains and the earth for long distances. I use my drum as a vehicle... it is the horse that I ride into the other world. There, in my trance... I have visions of pleasant people, helpful animals, and beautiful flowers."

Alexander Tavakay

Tuva is in central Asia, in the southern regions of Siberia and on the northern edge of Mongolia. Three mountain ranges—the Sayan, Altai and Tannu Ola—form its natural borders and have long isolated this remote area and its people. The former Soviet Union closed Tuva to the outside world for nearly half a century. Numerous monuments and burial sites of the nomadic Scythian (Kazylgan) culture remain, tracing Tuvan roots to an ancient lineage.

For millennia, nomadic Tuvans have tended their herds of reindeer, camels, yaks, sheep, goats and horses. Traditionally, they have lived in yurts, felt-covered circular tents, that can be moved to follow the cattle's seasonal pastures. Tuvan nomads have a mixed ethnic heritage, reflecting the ancient powers that dominated this part of Asia. Ghengis Khan's mother is said to be Tuvan. They have persisted in speaking their own language of Turkic origin even while being ruled by the Mongols and the Manchus. Today, after decades of Soviet domination, they still remember their sacred music in healing traditions.

"My grandfather was a great shaman. But under Stalin he was killed for his spiritual practices. The sky is our father and the earth our mother. I call the spirits of the rivers and the mountains to sanctify our home."

ALEXANDER TAVAKAY
TUVAN SHAMAN

"Shamanism is sometimes regarded as the oldest religion in the world, possibly even preceding the migration of Siberian peoples into North America over the land bridge that existed between Asia and America and which is now the Bering Strait," according to ethnomusicologist Bernard Kleikamp.

The strong relationship between Tuvan shamanism and nature stems from the Tuvan nomadic way of life. In the 17th century, Lamaism

Above and opposite page: Alexander Tavakay performing "Calling Animal Helpers."

was brought from Mongolia into Tuva. It influenced the spiritual life of the people and was absorbed into shamanic practices. This new form of religion flourished until the Soviet revolution, in 1917. Following the destruction of Buddhist monasteries and trading centers, a decade of internal political struggle and, finally, Stalin's undisputed leadership of the Communist party, indigenous shamanic practices were publicly banned for more than half a century.

In 1991, a group of ten shamans and scholars from Europe, the United States and Canada, in association with the Foundation for Shamanic Studies in California, were invited by the Tuvan government to participate in the country's first International Conference on Shamanism. The conference took place in the capital city of Kyzel — in the old Communist headquarters, a satisfying irony. Tuvan shaman Alexander Tavakay participated in this historic event.

ALEXANDER TAVAKAY IN KYZEL, THE CAPITAL OF TUVA

Alexander, now nearly eighty, learned how to call his helper spirits and perform shamanic rituals by watching his mother practice when he was a boy. He has been a professional actor for 40 years. Under the relentless scrutiny of the Communist regime, the theater was the only refuge in which he and others could openly perform indigenous shamanic practices. Now he practices shamanic rituals without fear of persecution. No longer performing treatments in secret, he cares for those within his community who are ill.

Tavakay treats many culture-specific illnesses and specializes in one: He is often called by families to speak to the spirit of a deceased relative. As an interpreter between worlds, Tavakay resolves lingering psychological issues from the past and satisfies the needs of both the living and the dead. This is one part of his therapeutic skills, which also include masterful drumming, the utterance of specific animal sounds, and the singing of songs of invocation and healing. He also draws upon his finely tuned psychic abilities.

This shaman is garbed in sound. Attached to the back of his red, white and blue ritual costume *(ala khuyak)* are rattles, rings, metal strips and bells. With every move and dance-like step he clanks and jangles. He holds a large red drum *(dungur)* and strikes it evenly with a felt-covered stick *(orbu)*. With voice, costume and drum, he summons his helping spirits and self-induces a trance state. He prepares for a journey to the other world. He sounds animal calls and sacred healing songs. Ribbons and strips of cloth cascading down his back represent snakes, protective spirits. The metal strips and bells hanging from his cloak frighten away evil spirits and prevent their interruptions. He collects evil and disease in his drum, and then beats the drum so that the evil will fly away.

"The Tuvans take the drum for a horse and the drumstick for a whip. The drum has to be tamed and trained in an enlivening ceremony, after which only the shaman may use the drum, for the spirit of the drum may cause death to another person who took it."

Bernard Kleikamp

The circular wooden frame of Alexander's dungur measures about seventy centimeters across. Unlike the drums of shamans in western Tuva, there are no symbolic drawings on the red-painted skin heads of Alexander's drum.

"Every Tuvan shaman has his own helping animal spirits. With his voice he may call on aid from these animals or make other animal sounds that are used for specific purposes. A cuckoo call to quiet a child, a raven's crow to scare away bad people and an owl's hoot to calm the cattle."

Alexander Tavakay

Tavakay summons whatever will best aid in the healing of his patients through sound and songs, the beat of his drum and sacred intent. His spiritual responsibility, to make a member of his community well again, guides him.

Track 9
Alexander Tavakay
"Calling Animal Helpers"
This song invokes helping spirits. He calls the cuckoo, raven and the owl while shaking the sound makers attached to his costume and beating his drum. This ritual is commonly used to heal children.

CHAPTER TEN

Pointing Father
Spiritual Baptist Immigrants from Saint Vincent Island

"Serve the LORD with gladness:
come before his presence with singing"
Psalm 100

Spiritual Baptist churches dot the small Caribbean island of Saint Vincent, standing ready to save souls through the life-giving baptismal waters of Jesus Christ. Spiritual Baptists are known in Saint Vincent as the most African of the Christian denominations, for historically they blend the Methodism of 19th-century British Revivalist missionaries with African religious philosophies. "The Converted," or "The Penitent," as they are sometimes called, are known as powerful spirit-workers, able to "see" and heal with special gifts that flow from their continued focus on God.

Vincentian immigrants in the United States also include numerous Spiritual Baptist faithful, who bring their traditions to the new setting, writes ethnographer Wallace W. Zane. Sunday church services last for six and seven hours, with additional meetings during the week in homes and hospitals for the sick and the suffering. Beautiful singing begins every Baptist prayer meeting, and music washes the congregation for the entire length of the service, throughout prayers, sermons and spiritual work. "With music we entertain the spirit to come in and take over your problems from you," explains the pastor, or Pointing Father, of one U.S. church, who wishes to remain anyonymous to maintain the privacy of his community,

"We never ask nobody to come and join us; but somebody will get a dream, somebody will get a vision, and he come to us and we baptise him in the river and put him out on the Mournin' Ground to pray and fast and wait for the Lord to send him a sign. . ."

Earl Lovelace, novelist

This spiritual pilgrim, dressed in blue and blindfolded, is carried into the sea on the back of her church sister to be baptized.

Above: A Thanksgiving Table in a Vincentian Spiritual Baptist church is laden with fruit and vegetables to praise God for His many merciful blessings.

New church members are joyfully baptised by the congregation in a nearby river or in the sea, a symbol of the River Jordan where John first baptised Jesus. The newly-baptised then go through the ritual called "Mourning," known as a healing time among Baptists. Mourning is a period of seclusion and fasting lasting seven days or more, sanctioned by the vision of Ezekiel, whom God told to "Go, shut thyself within thine house."

The mourner, once washed and anointed, thus becomes a pilgrim on a spiritual journey to cleanse away sins and be healed in the Spirit. The period is a time of trial, an ordeal, during which mourners become ritually purified. They are led on their spiritual journey by their Pointing Mother and Pointing Father, the leaders of the Spiritual Baptist community. "A lot are sick and come [to] receive healing," explains the Pointer. "A lot come who just want to be closer to God."

"Pointing" has to do with "pointing people in the spirit," says the Pointer Father whose church I attended. "It means to send them on, showing them the way of salvation. We are sending them on to talk to God, as they want to talk to God. The problems they have, they can't tell us, but they can tell God."

The Mourning room is inside the church itself, and will be covered in verses from scripture, seals, paintings and spirit-writing. Here the pilgrims will begin their healing journey. "In the room it is like a hospital, like a healing school. We call it a mystery school. They might come in for something and get something different," said the Pointing Father.

Many people receive gifts on their spiritual journey; bells, flags or ranks in the church. A Pointer might be given his or her rank in the Mourning room. "I became a Pointer by praying hard, studying hard, focusing my mind on God, and mourning. I mourn a lot. The more I go into the mourning room, the more they give me something to do. I do it, so when I get back I receive a higher gift," said Pointer.

One of this Pointer's gifts is his powerful voice, an instrument he uses to give sermons, lead prayers and call out hymns. Some of the songs he sings he has received on his spiritual travels, as a gift from God. He says that songs can come to save you when you are blocked in the spirit. "When you go to mourn, the burden can be too great for you. One song can come and sing to you and you hum that tune for yourself; it can be a door that comes wide open, so the song is a key. The song can help you go through. Every song we sing is a key for somebody." Not mere melodies, songs for the Spiritual Baptists are spiritual keys to help people along the road to healing and salvation. The Pointing Father leans over to tap my bible. "Psalm 98 tells us, 'O Sing unto the Lord a new song; for he hath done marvelous things...'"

The pilgrim's journey is intense, and mourners may confront both good and evil, and see angels and demons. "Music in the mourning room is important," explains the Pointer. "It helps the person to go through. With music we bring their mind into God."

SHOUTING

"O Clap your hands, all ye people; shout unto God with the voice of triumph"
Psalm 47

The Shouting, or final service, in the Mourning ritual, is a time of joyous spiritual rebirth. "Shouting is rejoicing for the one who went out seeking and bringing good news back," smiles the Pointer.

Some spiritual offices are charged with keeping up the "rejoicing," according to Wallace Zane. A "captain" takes over the singing when church members' "rejoice in the spirit." Here, the congregation may take a short collective spirit journey, with the captain guiding the "ship" to its destination and generally determining the nature and intensity of the spiritual experience. This "rejoicing" is accompanied by rhythmic vocalizations which are singular and movingly beautiful. Here, the captain is singing with a single voice reaching two tones. Other voices add melodies and embellishments.

Written by Elizabeth McAlister Ph.D.

Track 10 Point Father
"Shouting Ritual for Healing Spirit and Body, Doption Section." The "Doption," which is part of the Shouting Ritual facilitates spiritual and physical healing among immigrant Spiritual Baptists. Recorded in New York City in August, 1996. The members of the Spiritual Baptist Church wish no acknowledgement for themselves and instead give praise to God, the Almighty Creator.

A Spiritual Baptist Pointing Father poses with a new daughter in the church. She has just been baptized in the ocean and now adorns herself in white. He wears the long robes, belt and head tie signaling his rank as Pointer.

CHAPTER ELEVEN

Mara'akame
Huichol Peyote Shaman from Mexico

"The shamans, with their long flowing hair, their tobacco gourds and their ability to cure and to sing, are thought to resemble the gods."

Huichol legend

Huichol Indians believe that they are the mirrors of the gods. In their daily actions and rituals, they reflect a sacred vision of the universe, both physically and spiritually. Esoteric teachings from deities help maintain balance in the world and within their communities.

Huichol Indians hold the *mara'akame* — shaman priests, or "living gods" — in highest esteem. They are the keepers of the collective sacred knowledge that extends back to the beginning of time.

"These Indians are named by the Mexicans *Los Huicholes*, a corruption of *Vishalika*, or *Virarika*, as they call themselves, the word signifying "doctors" or "healers," wrote Norwegian explorer and naturalist Carl Lumholtz.

Over centuries, the Huichol Indians have preserved their culture, despite Aztec and Spanish conquests, efforts to convert them to Christianity and the continual flow of many races of foreigners through their homeland. Their protective borders continue to contract every year.

Huichols speak an Uto-Aztecan dialect and have a complex society where religion pervades every aspect of their life. It incorporates sacred art and music, shamanic practices, ritualized hunts and the ingestion of *hikuri,* or peyote.

About 16,000 Huichol Indians live in the Sierra Madre Mountains of central western Mexico, in the states of Jalisco and Nayarit. In the last three decades, the Mexican government has tried to integrate Los Huicholes into mainstream Mexican society, disturbing their traditional lifestyle and forcing a greater dependence on currency. Families migrate to the coast of Nayarit to find jobs, but their presence in contemporary Mexico is not always respected, and the long periods spent away from their home villages further threaten the survival of the Huichol way of life.

Hikuri

Hikuri (peyote) is a hallucinogenic, mandala-shaped cactus. It is sacred and ritually consumed by the Huichol Indians. "It attunes them to the *eeyalhlree neeahrhi'tuahlri*—the heart of God, which is lent to them while in a the peyote state, the source of the mara'akame's power," says Susan Eger, field director for the Foundation for the Indians of the Sierra.

Above: A Huichol mara'akame praying beside sacred waters.

A mara'akame chanting and petitioning the gods for healing.

Huichol woman making tesquino (maize beer).

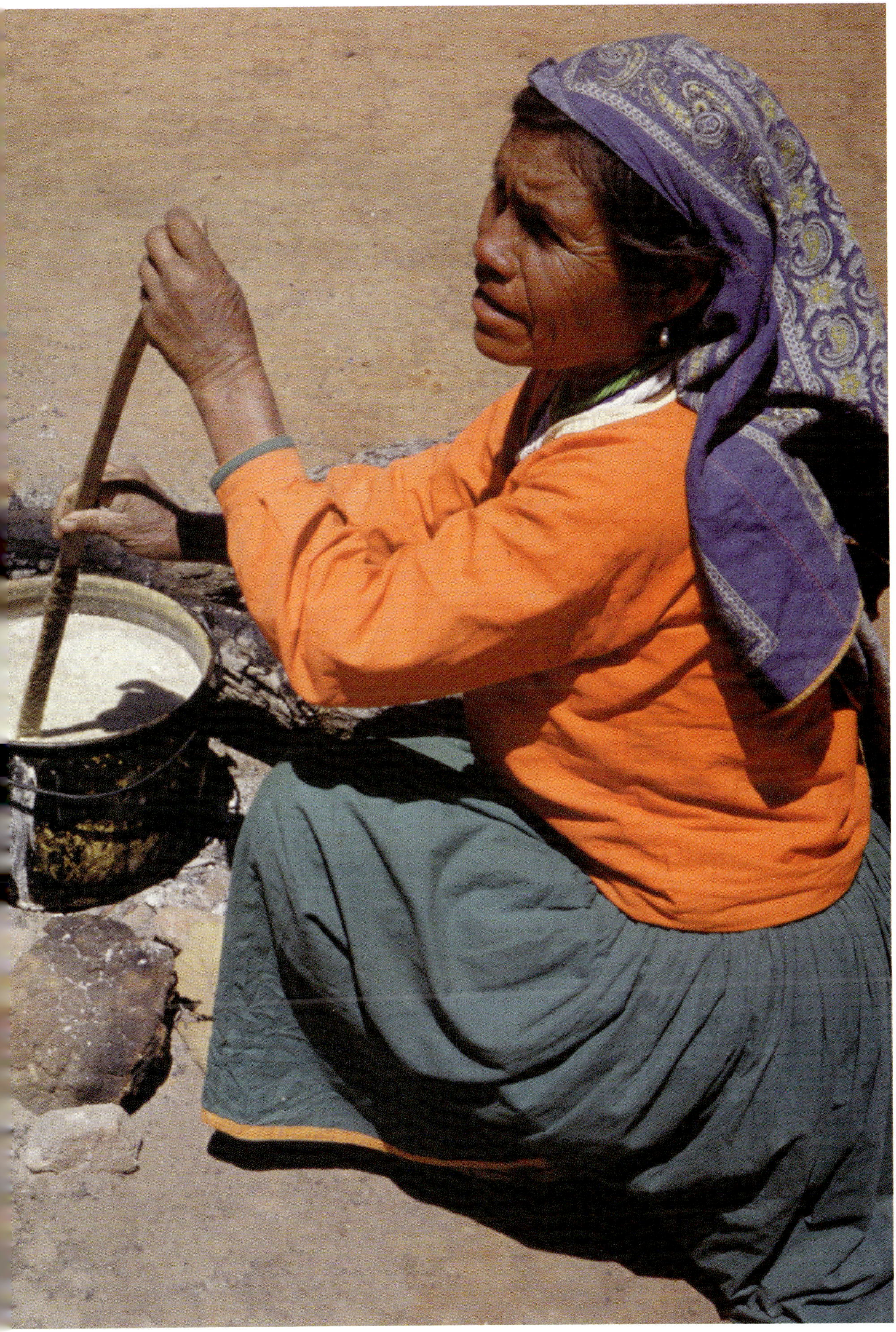

MARA'AKAME

"When I was a little boy I was able to see in this special way, and I remember well," said Eligo, a Huichol yarn painter. "My father once took me to a Huichol rancho near our home. I was sitting next to a grain bin listening to a mara'akame sing and I could see color visions of all that he was singing about."

In Huichol society, both men and women can become a mara'akame. The most experienced are the *Contadoras*. "I want to see into the visionary world," said Don Jose, "to make good yarn paintings of the gods, spirits and powers who teach the mara'akate how to heal and conduct ceremonies."

Over two thirds of the Huichol men are *mara'kate* (plural of mara'akame). Fewer women endeavor to be among the initiated and often marry a shaman. The large number of Huicholes that become shamans can be attributed to lifelong intensive exposure to the metaphysical aspects of Huichol life and culture through its peyote-based practices.

> The peyote experience begins in infancy, through the breast milk of the mother. "Nursing mothers are required to partake of peyote if they or their husbands are active members of the community," reports Susan Eger.

A mara'akame demonstrates unusual intuitive abilities early in life. He has vivid dreams, receives messages from deities or has overcome a serious illness. He exhibits special talents in art or music and often has excellent skills in both. A person's entire being must desire to become a mara'akame and nothing else. Throughout life, there are difficult tests and levels to pass through, requiring intense practice. It is a lifelong commitment to cure illness and to help their communities make sense out of natural disasters (earthquakes, lightning, drought), sickness and the infringing modern world.

CANTOS DE CURACION

The mara'akame learns to chant and sing sacred Huichol myths and *cantos de curacion*, songs for curing. In healing rituals, the shaman always chants, usually without instrumental accompaniment. Other ritual chants are performed a capella, with accompanying voices, or with a *sonaja* rattle made from a gourd-like fruit from the *tecomate* tree, or with drums, violin and guitars.

Shamans are skilled in a traditional stringed instrument called the "bow drum," a hunting bow that serves as a musical instrument "by tapping the bowstring with a wooden-tipped arrow and using the mouth as a sound chamber," says anthropologist Peter Furst.

The mara'akame plays the *tepu,* a three-legged vertical upright log drum. The *tepu* has a deerskin head and resounds loudly when played. Huichol mythology and symbolism is connected with the drum, allowing only the mara'akame to play it. Tatewari, the Great Mara'akame, made the first drum and "taught its use and meaning to the divine ancestors, and with its beat cured the sick children of the ancient Huichols," said Furst.

The Huichols associate illness with specific deities. For example a soreness in the face or a fever, is called *nealika itali* (bed in face), and the God of Fire (the source of all heat) is said to be making his bed in the patient's face. Bronchitis, is called *moyaeli* (plumes). The cough indicates that the illness is caused by the God of Wind and of hikuli. Ailments of the foot are called *rikua* (the word for rattling objects or bells), similar to the sound of a walking deer. The disease is attributed to Great Grandfather Deer-Tail. Colic is called *rukuli* (gourd bowl), because the stomach is consid-

A mara'akame chanting and petitioning the gods for healing.

ered a food bowl. The Goddess of the Western Clouds sends this affliction. In all instances, either grains of corn, charcoal, an arrow point or various objects must be removed from the site of illness.

The gods come down at night during the rainy season to make people ill, either for their own reasons or dispatched by a bad shaman seeking to destroy an enemy. The conception that illness is caused by sorcery is common.

"THE GODS BRING THE SICKNESS"

The Gods send the sickness when they are angry. Maybe it was disharmony in the village. The elders could not agree which god should receive the offering. Now we are sick and I must cure this illness.

Juan, a mara'akame

Chants and songs pray to the deity and request healing. "The creator gave me the gift to treat the chest and stomach," said the mara'akame.

Track 11
Mara'akame
"Song for Petitioning the Gods for Healing"
This is a rare field recording of a Huichol peyote shaman from the 1940s. This mara'akame is petitioning the gods for healing.

CHAPTER TWELVE

Jorge K'in
Lacandon Mayan Shaman

"In the jungle we find our gods; our dead people. There live the plants that heal us, the water and the animals that feed us. That's why we pray and sing there every day."

*Chan' Kin Viejo, to'ohil
(The Great One)*

The Mayan civilization was one of the richest to ever grace the earth. Long before the birth of Christ or Buddha, the Maya had developed a cosmology and a way of life that was pervasively spirtual. Their origins date back to the Olmec culture, three millenia ago, but today, less than 500 true Maya survive in the State of Chiapas, in the Mexican rainforest. They are called the *Lacandones* or *Hach Winik* — meaning "True Men" or "The Original People," as they call themselves.

According to linguist Robert Bruce, who lived among the Lacandon for many years, the term *Lacandon* (also written *Lakandon* and *Lacandones*) is the Maya plural for "those who set up stone idols" *(ah akan-tun-oob),* a name was given to them by nearby Christianized Maya who viewed them as pagan idol-worshippers. The Spaniards called them *Acantunes* (pagans or wild Indians) and called their jungle home *El Acantun.* El Acantun became, over time, *El Lacandon,* and the people who lived there became the Lacandones.

The Lacandones escaped extermination during the Spanish Conquest, unlike their Maya neighbors who were either assimilated, forced to convert to Christianity, or slaughtered. Mayan literature and libraries were burned, leaving few materials extant today.

Contact with Protestant churches over the past forty years has censored numerous ritual practices. As a result, the Lacandon are forgetting their mythic tales, prayers and songs, and more of their original sacred links are being severed. Modern-day attempts to nationalize the Lacandon have failed, but the contemporary engines of commerce — loggers, multinational corporations, and cattle ranchers — now threaten the Lacandon way of life and the *Selva Lacandon* (Mexican rain forest, Lacandon jungle).

Intimately linked with nature, the Lacandon rely on agriculture, *milpi* (corn fields) and natural resources from forest plants and animals to survive. The people harvest corn, chile, cacao, and avocados. Their diet is complemented by fish, venison, squirrel, monkey, and various birds. Tobacco is cultivated, and pottery is crafted for sale at San Cristobal de las Casas or in the archeological zones

Above: Mayan Ruins of Palenque.

of Palenque, Konakax, Yaxchilan and Bonampak.

The northern group of Lacandones are the most traditional, although they have been exposed to modern technologies and occidental medicine. Lacandones value Western medicine, which they believe is sent to them with the permission of the gods, and yet are careful to avoid any semblance of conflict between new and traditional curing rituals. Curing ceremonies take place in temples, but Western treatments occur privately, in their living quarters.

Little separation is made between humanity, nature and the gods, as this relationship between all three provides the material and spiritual foundation of the Lacandon culture. Life depends on this flow.

Lacandon songs used in curing ceremonies include calling on the great spirit of the *tigre* (jaguar) and boar. All three animals exhibit incredible strength and ability to survive.

"I have recorded two ancient oral recitations, songs about *el Tigre*," said Elliot Diamond, M.D., who travelled to Palenque with medical anthropologist Joan Halifax to record Jorge K'in during a benefit concert for the Lacandon Maya in Chiapas.

"The songs illustrate the importance of the Tigre in the spiritual and everyday life of the Lacandon. Jorge sings about the time when man turned into the Tigre and back, at will. It is about the union of Tigre and rainforest that added so much vitality to their survival."

JORGE K'IN

The name *K'in* means many things: sun, day, prophecy and prophet. It is one of the four most common names among the Lacandon Maya and has been shared by numerous leaders and shamans over the centuries. Such is the case with one of the last Hach Winik in Mexico, the Lacandon healer Jorge K'in, now nearly eighty years old.

Jorge K'in in the Mexican rainforest in Chiapas, Mexico.

"Man's power to transform himself was important. It is used to bring power into healing ceremonies," continued Diamond.

"When we were staying with the Lacandon, we could hear the jaguar at night…the ferocious but sweet sounds echoing and making its mark," recalled Diamond.

The Song of The Tigre

The Tigre is able to see at night or in the dark. He has powerful eyesight and is able to aid in healing. This is valuable to Lacandon curing ceremonies. "I know a lot of Tigre songs for healing," offered Jorge K'in, and he began to sing…

Look at the Mountain, by foot

Flying and not flying, running

Only on the foot of the Tigre

Only on the mountain

Seen with the Tigre

He is like a person, but is a tigre,

Now back again as a person…

"I know many songs. but I like the Tigre song…it is beautiful. So there!" he laughed, "good songs, pure song, it is the Tigre spirit…"

Various illnesses afflict people in the rainforest, including malaria, internal parasites, infections and snake bite. Unexplained illnesses are often attributed to spiritual matters. The Lacandon shaman is also a specialist in ecstasy, that state of freedom that allows them to move beyond the ordinary world, beyond pain and illness and death.

Death is thought to be simply a continuum; another porthole through which the soul can move. Jorge deals directly with the gods, demons, spirit animals and ancestors.

Track 12
Jorge K'in
"Song of the Tigre to Cure Jungle Illness"
This rare recording of the gentle voice of Jorge K'in was recorded in the Mexican rainforest. He sings a song to the tigre (jaguar) whose power is used in healing rituals.

Above: Mayan Ruins of Palenque.

CHAPTER THIRTEEN

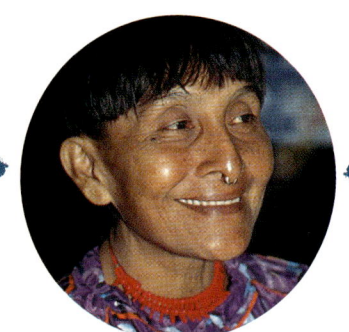

Néle Buna Inayenikidili
Kuna Indian Seer of the San Blas Islands

My companions and I left Panama City near dawn. We flew southeast to the San Blas Islands off Panama's Atlantic coast. Our rickety plane squeaked, rocked and sputtered through torrents of rain. That it flew at all was a miracle. An hour later, we landed on a muddy strip opposite the Kuna Island of Ustupu. We had come to meet with a *néle* (seer).

The Kuna Indians

The Kuna Indians (or Cuna) are one of Panama's three indigenous groups. With a present-day population of about 30,000, the Kuna maintain a highly organized, independent culture. They trace their beginnings to Mount Tacaruna in southeastern Panama, but linguistic comparisons suggest that the Kuna most likely migrated from South America, driven north by intertribal warfare.

In Panama, their villages were attacked by Spanish explorers and pirates. Other European explorers, such as Sir Francis Drake, William Dampier, and Lionel Wafer also paid frequent visits to the isthmus. In each case, the Kuna eventually drove their enemies and foreign visitors out, until survey teams and military expeditions came to the San Blas Islands early in this century, to set up military posts and build the Panama Canal.

The Kuna region includes 365 islands along the coastal mainland. The Kuna are protective of their territory, the *Kuna Yala,* and its boundaries are recognized by the Republic of Panama as an autonomous Kuna region. The Kunas speak their own language and have a sophisticated belief system and cosmology.

Ustupu

As we got off the plane, swarms of gnats and mosquitoes attacked. Bug repellent was no match. Our guides Ric and Marie-France Hajovsky led us to a huge motorized dugout canoe where we met Leno, our Kuna interpreter. We fled the bug-infested mainland; the cool sea breeze blew away the hordes of insects. We passed an uninhabited island. "The néles are buried there," said Leno. "Even dead, their spirits watch over Ustupu and protect us."

Eight hundred people live on the island of Ustupu. The men fish and the women tend their children and manage the house. Life is simple; it is

Above: Néle Buna Inayenikidili

A dugout canoe on the beach of Ustupu.

ruled by the sun. People sleep when the sun goes down and awaken at sunrise. Gulls, an occasional lizard and, at night, vampire bats constitute the only wildlife on the island. For sustenance, the Kuna depend on the sea, Central American trade boats, and native vegetable farms on the mainland.

A bustling town square hosts a variety of activities and sports. Villagers hold nightly political meetings in a government hut nearby. A modest monument occupies a central place in the square in honor of Ustupu's most famous néle. *Néles* are seers and healers. They are held in high esteem for their wisdom and healing powers.

Tomas De Leon, the *Saila De Ustupu* (chief of Ustupu), offered his hand. He grants permission for any foreign research or activity on the island. Half a day — and a substantial fee — later, the arrangements were in place, and we could visit the néle.

BUNA INAYENIKIDILI

Buna Inayenikidili is a néle and midwife. She looks classically Kuna with high cheekbones and long nose, pierced with a gold ring. Her legs and forearms are tightly wrapped in multicolored beads, highlighting her soft violet cotton dress. Her short jet-black hair, dark eyes and air of confidence give her a dignified and peaceful countenace.

Néle Inayenikidili is a small woman in her mid-40s. Patients see her for a diagnosis, after which she either prescribes botanical medicine or sends the patient to a *absogedi,* or *maestro,* a specialist in medicine songs.

"We divide the underworld into eight layers *(pilis)*," she explained. "When someone is sick, they can't find their *purba* (soul). An evil *poni* (spirit) has taken it to the underworld. I ask the *nuchus* (medicine dolls) to go and look for the purba. I can also travel there in spirit with them. The nuchu brings back a message from the underworld. It tells me where the purba is held captive. Now I know what illness my patient is suffering from and what the treatment will be."

A small box full of nuchus or *uabanéle* (in shamanic language) sat at her feet. Most of the painted figures wore hats. Each is possessed by a tutelary spirit that the néle petitions in her fight against evil spirits. Nuchus are anthropomorphic, although animal figures are occasionally found.

Nuchus are carved from balsa, cacao, liana (a vine), aji, and other semi-hardwoods. The wood is naturally imbued with its own guardian spirit, which is also incorporated into the nuchu. These protector figures possess great *kurgin* (power), a

Kuna nuchu dolls that possess kurgin (power).

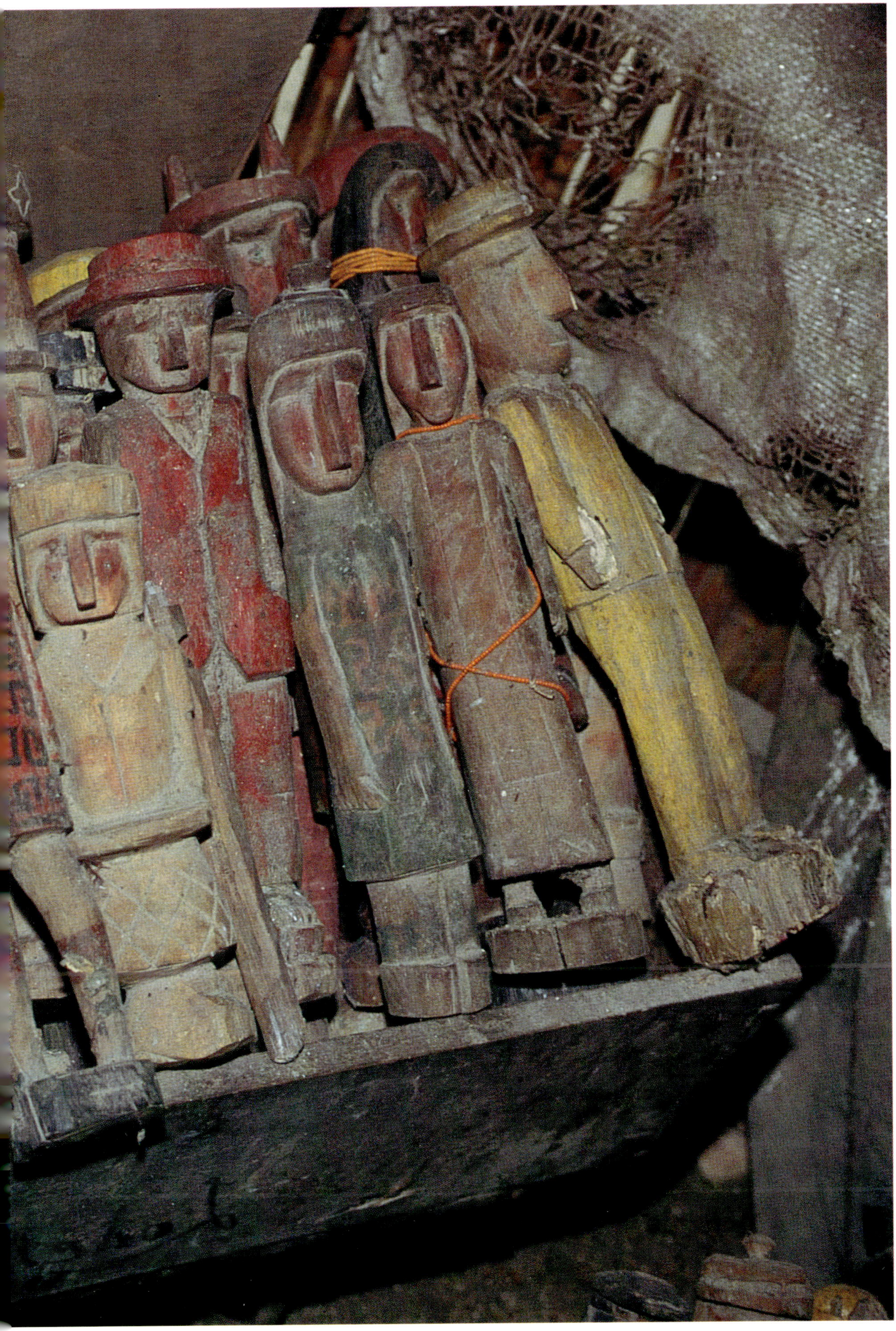

Pat Moffitt Cook and Buna Inayenikidili in the néle's hut.

Kuna concept of endowed strength. Kurgin is centered in the brain, but the word 'kurgin' can also mean brain or hat. These different-sized carvings can depict mythological beings, ancestors (néles and their relatives) or other persons that the Kuna perceive as strong: police, soldiers or a diseased *Saila;* Christian figures such as Jesus, Mary or angels; or pop-culture icons like Superman.

The Kuna believe that each person possesses a specific kind of kurgin. That is why some people are good hunters or artists, or become *sailas* or néles. Kurgin can be transferred into an object that a néle sings over. The object becomes 'supercharged' with one type of kurgin and given to a person deficient in that type.

"Sometimes my patient takes a bath in medicine water," said Buna Inayenikidili. (A kurgin-bearing object can be soaked for several hours or days before bathing.) "Sometimes I tell them to eat small pieces of the nuchus wood. This also cures."

Energy accumulates in the patina of special objects as well. The staff of a néle or absogedi is imbued with great energy and power. The staff also symbolizes high status in the community. Néles use it in curing ceremonies.

A purba is stolen when a Kuna is startled or frightened. At that moment, he or she becomes vulnerable to evil spirits that are always lurking, waiting to drag a soul into the underworld. The result is serious illness. Not all illnesses are caused by abduction of the purba; minor ills are caused by evil spirits simply wishing to cause human pain. These illnesses can be cured with botanical medicine (sung over before harvesting), medicinal chants and baths containing wooden medicine from the nuchus.

"With the aid of the nuchus, a néle can diagnose a patient's illness and prescribe the appropriate medicine. This is accomplished either by a house call, in which the nuchus are consulted in the patient's home, or via long distance," said our guide, Ric Havjosky.

"If a house call is not possible then the patient holds a nuchu for a while so that the nuchu understands the nature of the illness and then sends it to the néle who consults with it before making a diagnosis."

Above: The néle singing a shamanic chant.

Following a diagnosis, the néle may send the patient to an absogedi or maestro, who specializes in specific healing songs (for headaches, mental illness, fevers and other culture-specific diseases). He sings and chants sophisticated, ancient medicinal songs that continue for as long as four days. In some cases he is charging the nuchus, for they must return to the underworld layer and free the purba from the evil spirits. His song is his (and his ancestors') concentration of kurgin, extreme power to battle evil. In the end, the nuchu returns the soul to the patient, who then becomes well.

"While being petitioned by the absogedi to confront evil spirits, the nuchus are reminded to take their hats (kurgin) with them," explained Ric. "The hats contain the burning *aji* (chili pepper), which can be released to blind and confuse evil spirits. When the patient has been reunited with his purba and has recovered, the nuchus are told to stand down, whereupon they become dormant until the next time they are required."

The néle has a repetoire of songs that imbue medicine (charge it) and communicate with nuchus. Objects (rocks, a shark's tooth, a plastic bottle, or animal bones) can become medicine, to be placed in the patients home, ingested or held. The néle's song contains kurgin that transfers to these inanimate objects and transforms them into tools of healing.

Track 13
Néle Buna Inayenikidili
"Charging the Medicine Dolls"
Buna Inayenikidili singing over a box of medicine objects and nuchu dolls in her hut on the Kuna island, Ustupu. Recorded June, 1996.

The néle's medicine box.

CHAPTER FOURTEEN

Anselmo Palma Cruz
Tarahumara Owiruame from the Sierra Madres

"I sing so sadness can go away. Sadness is the cause of sickness."

Anselmo
An Owiruame (Medico Tradicional)

The Tarahumara Indians, who call themselves the Raramuri or "light feet," live in Mexico, 1,100 kilometers northwest of Mexico City. Their homeland straddles the Sierra Madre continental divide, an area that covers some 35,000 square kilometers in southwestern Chihuahua. Rugged terrain and poor communication make it difficult to estimate the Raramuri population, but as the state's largest indigenous group, they number between 50,000 and 75,000.

The Raramuri can be traced to those prehistoric peoples who spoke Uto-Aztecan languages. "The speakers of these languages have occupied this area for several thousand years," says anthropologist Wick Miller. Today the Raramuri language remains their first language despite centuries of social and religious change through contact with *Chabochis*, "the whiskered ones," or non-Indians.

The Raramuri made their first contact with Europeans in the 16th century. The Spanish conquest, the discovery of silver in the southeast aboriginal Raramuri territory, and the establishment of Catholic and Jesuit missions led to 400 years of Indian exploitation. The Indians were subjected to forced conversion to Christianity and suffered widespread mortality from foreign diseases. The Raramuri shrank in number; they were forced to live near missions and in regulated areas. Over time, they assimilated aspects of Christian ritual into their own complex religion and cosmology.

"Contemporary Raramuri religion and cosmology reflect the influence of Catholicism, but the missionaries have had more impact on ritual than on religious belief itself. The Raramuri considered many of the Christian rituals to have a material efficacy, especially in preventing illness."

William Merrill, anthropologist
The Smithsonian Institution

ANSELMO CRUZ

"I go and see the sick. I place three crosses with some tesquino *(maize beer), not much, just a little. We use violin and guitar. Someone else plays. I don't. I have to work with the Christ. I have to sing the music so no one is sad. It is like prayer."*

Anselmo

Above: The village center in Anselmo's village, Huillorare.

Maize is the principal component of the Raramuri diet; therefore maize and its liquid derivative *suguri* are sacred. Legend asserts that God created suguri for humans to rejoice, be together and work together. Suguri is based on sprouted and fermented corn. Another name for this drink is *tesguino*, the Spanish word for Raramuri maize beer. It is an important part of Raramuri life and holds a prominent place in healings.

Anthropologist Merrill reported, "from the gourd dipper he (Cruz) administered three sips of maize beer to his patient and then dipped the spoon in the beer to make crosses on Calistro's (his patient's) head and shoulders and then on his elbows, touching the spoon to his own chest before replacing it in the cup."

In Chihuahua, several recognized healers practice among the Tarahumara Indians who use song, beer and the *sukristo,* or crucifix, to cure the sick. These healers are called *Owiruame*.

A true Owiruame has the ability to control unseen worlds outside the human realm, and is further empowered by God's blessings. The power to heal is related to heritage, but in some cases a born healer does not have to have blood ties to receive the status of Owiruame. To be recognized in the community and to show power, the healer must have his blessed sukristo that defends him and serves as a healing instrument. He must be able to communicate with special plants such as *Hikuli* (peyote), because it is essential to his healing work.

Owiruame Anselmo

"I was born on June 15, in 1943, in a place called Romeachi, but since I was a small child I lived in Huillorare," said Anselmo. "My father was also born in Romeachi. I am married and have two sons and three daughters. They are all married now."

> "I am a healer. It was given to me. At first I went with him [his father], he taught me the herbs and all about the work. The family must continue the work, he said to me. I'm teaching my son now.

His mother also knows; her parents taught her. The music was first made by them, the ancient Raramuri. I don't know who taught them. I only know the one who taught me."

"I go and see the sick. I have to sing the music so no one is sad. It is like a prayer. Before there were no strings for the violin or the guitar. I guess they used animal sounds."

Anselmo Palma Cruz in the front seat at a community meeting.

Happiness and Hygiene are Keys to Good Health

For the Raramuri people, to be in good health is to be happy. Sickness takes happiness away and makes the Raramuri sad. When serious issues emerge in the community, joking and laughter arise to prevent development of impending sadness. To talk publicly about sad issues or cause crying in other community members would mean to sink everyone into the same sadness. People would then become ill. Such behavior among Raramuri shows a lack of education.

Headaches, diarrhea and tuberculosis are thought to begin with sadness, not the sickness itself. The sources are generally fright, charm (bewitchment), trauma, loss, financial problems and personal needs. These sadnesses always turn into symptoms of illness, physical discomfort and, eventually, death.

The Owiruame jokes with his patients and onlookers, contrasting (in the Raramuri's opinion) with the solemnity of the *meztizo* (mixed-race) healers, or the superficial joy or seriousness of doctors and nurses. Parties and games abound in times of need. These celebrations are not intended to attract tourists, or serve as an excuse to get drunk. They represent the timeless ritual of communication with life — "the joy that keeps us alive," said one Raramuri.

Poor hygiene also causes illness. Sexually transmitted diseases appeared with the arrival of foreigners centuries ago. The concept of filth is associated with human conduct and morality, not with dust or mud from the earth. Illness travels through the air, and ill-meaning people can direct sickness toward someone. A sorcerer can breathe onto someone to make him sick. Mythical animals and frightening figures in dreams can also possess and make a person unwell.

"Then I have to examine to see where the sickness is — in the feet, the back or the head. I find the sickness and I use this blessed *sukristo* to pull out the pus and the bad blood. I don't take out stones, just bad blood with pus. I have to see them for three days for males, four days for females.

People get sick because others do them wrong; they are bewitched, or they are scared. My wife does some work but only I pull out the pus. I don't search for souls."

Anselmo

Crucifixes purchased from Chabochis are emblems of the status of a healer. Anselmo has received knowledge and permission from God to cure; thus he wears the crucifix around his neck. When this healing ability and power is given God also assigns one of his sons, "known as sukristo" — literally, Jesus Christ but distinct from the biblical figure of Christ — to help them. The sukristo is associated with the crucifix and has the power to transfer power and strength to both the healer and the patient.

Often, a figure is imposed upon the cross — an image of a saint or of Christ. But the cross is not worshipped by the Raramuri as a Christian symbol. It is more like an anthropomorphic entity that has the power to heal and change the direction of life when administered by an Owiruame.

"Catholicized Tarahumras make the sign of the cross when they approach peyote, greeting it as if it were a person. Before they are taken out for use, an offering of meat and tesguino must be made for them."

Victor Mendoza
Mexican scholar and researcher

Hikuli is a sacred plant used by the Owiruame. Like the sukristo, the Raramuri believe that hikuli plants possess human attributes and the power to cure.

"When Tata Dios [the Grandfather God] went to heaven, he left peyote behind as a remedy and talisman for the Tarahumara. The plant has four faces and sees everything, it is very powerful."

Victor Mendoza

Songs send sadness away and create a bridge between the Owiruame and his power to cure the sick in soul and body. The songs used in healing are not used at any other time in Raramuri life.

HEALING SONGS

"I use peyote. You have to honor him, feed him so he wants to help. He doesn't teach the song. He just helps heal. Everyone uses it but they don't like to say it."

Anselmo

The *Yumari* (songs) come from the Low Tarahumara and the High Tarahumara areas. These songs are interpreted during ceremonies for petitions, cures and giving thanks. Yumari are also played and sung during healing procedures; their interpreter is known as *Wikaraami*, singer. The singer performs in front of the *Awirachi*, the place where one dances. Crosses are placed and the offerings are made during the ceremony, according to its purpose. The singer may also play a rattle made of ash tree or oak.

Another group of healing songs, sung by the Owiruame, are called the *Rewisana*. They are only interpreted during healing procedures, so that the sick or charmed (bewitched) person heals quickly. Music is like food for sickness; you play for it so that it's fed and allows the sick to heal. Two or three of these pieces are played in one session. Rewisanas are reserved solely for healing and should not be played otherwise, according to the Tarahumara.

"Yes, people respect me, but not all. Of course the ones I heal do. I am the only healer in my town. Only I do this work. But, I am teaching others because when I am gone they will have to continue. This cannot end!"

Anselmo Cruz

Track 14
Anselmo Palma Cruz
"Chant for Healing Fever in Children"
Anselmo is chanting and playing a rattle to cure a child of fever. This track was recorded in his home town of Huillorare in November, 1996.

prayers, food a
and instrumen
afflicted perso
Koreans b
its are respon
sickness, early
Musok belief,
violent death,
not rest in pea
it, returning t
generations. C
with the peace
well as dead.
ancestors up
(parents, gran
great-grandpa
Unlike s
kangsinmu (sp
(hereditary mu
cure illness.
entertainment
that spirits w
ritual provide
relayed by the
concept of rec
Elaborate
performed by t

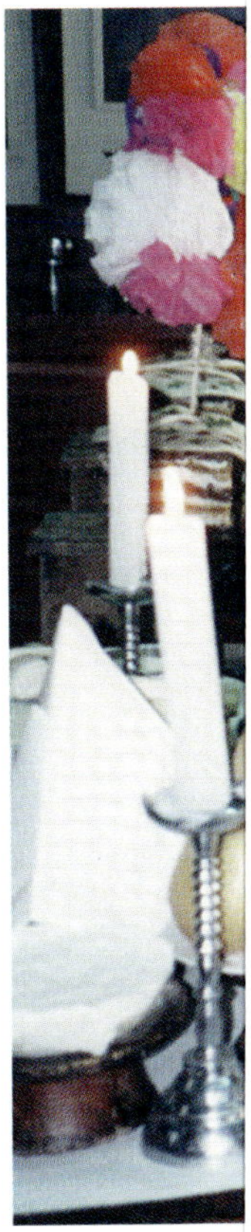

Shin Hye-gu, a

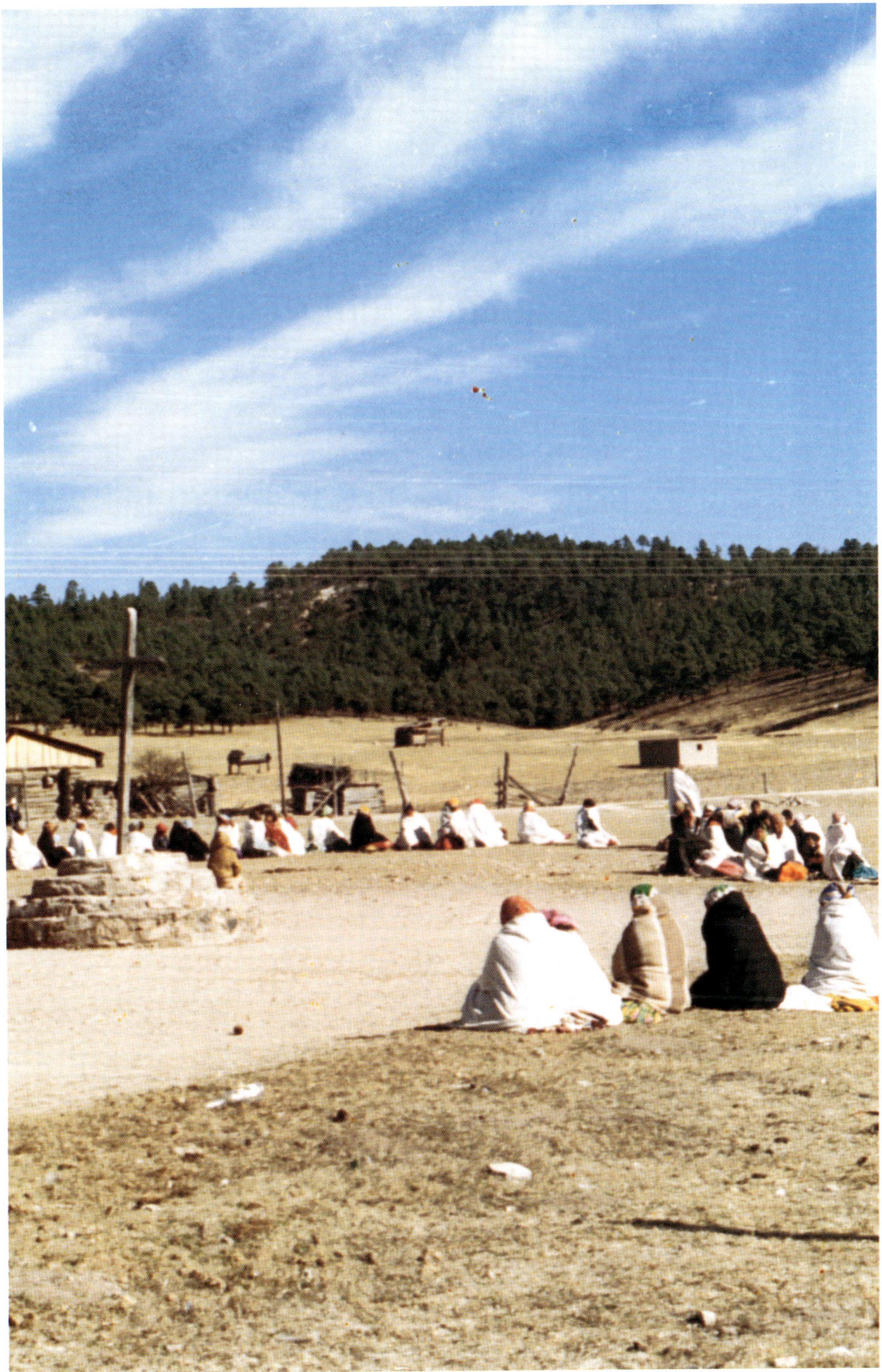

A community gathering in Huillorare. Healing rituals take place around the central cross.

Pak In-O, a paksu (spirit-possessed male shaman), singing and playing the changgo durin a kut (ritual) held at U-I-dong, Seoul.

bals) and *chong* (bells). A kangsinmu must also master the technique of calling spirits into his or her body and sending them away if the need arises.

MR. PAK IN-O

Mr. Pak In-O is a well established kangsinmu in Seoul. He became a mudang when he was a university student. He was seriously ill for about five years, during which time he simply refused to accept the fate of becoming a mudang. His family committed him to a mental hospital for a year, feeling ashamed and trying to deny the possibility of a family member becoming a mudang. After years of illness and confusion, he and his family submitted, and Mr. Pak reluctantly became a *paksu*, a male kangsinmu.

"I can diagnose the cause of suffering when a patient is brought to me because the spirits explain it to me. I have no medical knowledge or skill to cure a person, but I know that the spoken words I relay from the spirits to the patient, at the time of crisis, have curing power, if the patient follows the instructions with faith and devotion," reported Mr. Pak In-O.

Mr. Pak also remarked, "I often felt skeptical at the beginning of my work." But now, in his 50s, he has complete faith that the spirits have power beyond his comprehension. Mr. Pak is one of the many who believe that spirits have the power to diagnose and cure illness and misfortune.

Sometimes the cure is immediate and simple; at other times, the spirit suggests that a ritual be performed which requires elaborate and costly preparation. Musok believers follow this advice and sponsor a kut which may last from one to several days.

The music offered here to the listener is a song that calls the spirits to gather to cure illness and misfortune. Mr. Pak In-O sings, accompanying himself on the changgo, and Mr. Yang (a musician, not a mudang) plays the *p'iri* (bamboo oboe). The listener may also hear two neophytes singing along with Mr. Pak as a part of their learning process.

Written by Maria Seo Ph.C.

Track 15
Mr. Pak In-O
"Pujŏng Norae Karak"
(Song for Calling the Helping Spirits)
A paksu is a male kangsinmu (spirit-possessed mudang or shaman) who mediates between the worlds of spirits and human beings. He masters the technique of calling spirits into his body and sending them away. This song calls the spirits together to help exorcise a malevolent spirit causing illness and misfortune. Mr. Pak In-O sings, accompanying himself on the changgo, and Mr. Yang plays the piri heterophonically.

CHAPTER SIXTEEN

Steve Old Coyote
"Roadman" of the Native American Church

"The Coyote is the trickster."
Native American proverb

SUQUAMISH INDIAN RESERVATION

The Port Madison Indian Reservation spans 8000 acres of lush fir and cedar in Kitsap County, on the west coast of Washington state's Puget Sound. From its beaches and bluffs you can see across the Sound to Seattle, and on clear days, you can make out majestic Mount Rainier, 100 miles to the south.

The reservation is the home of the Suquamish Indian, famous because of chief Sealth, after whom Seattle was named. Early 19th-century European settlers called him Chief Seattle, and extended his name to the "emerald city."

Chief Sealth was one of the last spokesmen of the Paleolithic moral order. In 1855, the United States Government forced him to transfer his tribal lands to foreign settlers. He adopted his new name and the Christian religion in a profound effort to ensure protection for the Suquamish. Despite his efforts, however, alcoholism grew rampant and smallpox wiped out hundreds of his people. Religious and social oppression drove indigenous spiritual practices underground. Healing songs, rituals, drum-making and traditional teaching were performed in secret.

Commenting on that time in Suquamish history, the present-day "Roadman" Steve Old Coyote said, "We used our iron cooking pots for drums when they weren't watching us. We'd wet some leather and tie it over the opening. Then we'd stretch and tap the skin until the right sound came out."

Chief Sealth died in 1864 and was buried on the reservation in St. Peter's Catholic Church graveyard. Two traditional carved canoes, supported by great cedar posts, shade eight feet overhead. A giant oak, planted at his burial, canopies this symbolic monument. Local people and international tourists frequently stop by to pay their respects.

"One can almost hear the sacred sound-makers and rattles that are buried there in the earth with our Chief," said one Suquamish Indian.

NATIVE AMERICAN CHURCH

During the 1880s, when Native tribes were gathered onto reservations, a new Native American religion arose. With the loss of the buffalo, Native land and spiritual freedom, Native Americans found new ways to access great visions, healing and teachings. Within a decade, disinherited tribes all across America began to incorporate "medicine" from the desert cactus peyote, originally harvested in Northern Mexico, into sacred community meetings.

Today, the Native American Church "is recog-

Above: Steve Old Coyote

nized among some fifty tribes and incorporated as a distinct religion, with a membership said to be of some 200,000. The doctrines vary from area to area and in some may include Christian elements," wrote Joseph Campbell.

Peyote, an organic hallucinogen derived from the peyote cactus, is considered "medicine" in the Native American Church. Only church members may legally use it in the United States. As Campbell said, peyote is served to "recover knowledge from within of the spiritual ground of native life."

"I was born in Mankato, Minnesota in 1943. My mother and stepfather were Cree. My real father was a stranger in the night. We moved to South Dakota soon afterward because my stepfather was a migrant worker on ranches. We travelled a lot…too much, maybe. One year I went to three different schools. During most of my childhood I lived with my Grandma and my aunts and uncles. Once in a while I went back home. My Dad was an alcoholic and money was hard to come by. Home wasn't that pleasant for me…so one day I never went back. I hit the road to see what life was about.

Steve's tattooed hands tightening the leather drum head on the iron pot drum.

"THE ROADMAN"

Native American Church meetings and "sweat lodges" are led by a "roadman," who is a song and prayer leader. Drums and a peyote rattle accompany his prayer and healing songs.

Steve Old Coyote lives on the Suquamish land, which embraces Native Americans from different tribes. Steve moved to the reservation, where he and his wife Rita raised two children, now nearly grown, named James and Janaka, whose names mean keeper of the earth. Over time, Steve Old Coyote became one of the roadmen.

I learned a lot, including all the stories and songs I know," reminisced Steve.

As a community roadman, Steve leads sweat lodges for praying, for creating balance in the community through singing and for physical and spiritual healings. The songs are performed in varying order, depending upon the purpose of the meeting. Peyote is used for meetings, healing sessions and sweat lodges to open the consciousness of the roadman and the singers/participants. It is prepared by crushing the pod of the peyote cactus into a green powder, which is dampened and rolled into a little ball, to be held under the tongue. The medicine is also made into a tea. Whether the patients who are the subject of the roadman's healings also receive peyote is decided at the roadman's discretion.

"First we sing four songs," Steve explained. "The first song is for calling in the spirits. It's mellow and we call in all four spirits to help out. The second song identifies what's wrong, and in the third song we ask for the manifestation of healing. We sing the fourth song to give thanks to the creator for listening to us."

"I put the sick person in the sweat lodge. All of our energy and prayers must be given to him or her. We are not here for ourselves, like at other times… just for that person. First we lay the patient out…We make him as comfortable as we can. I tell him everything that is going to happen. Next I call the singers into the sweat lodge . . . they sit up on one side of the lodge. Then I call the other helpers to enter the lodge and sit up on the opposite side. Those people throw herbs, cedar, sage, sweet grass and sometimes pitch into the hot rocks during the different rounds. We choose the amount of medicine and what wood or herb to burn before the healing," said Steve.

KIDNEY AILMENT

Steve described treatment for a woman with a kidney ailment.

"First we gave her marsh tea. I told her to drink a gallon of it in one day. When she was done we had a meeting. We rolled her over on her left side and started drumming there. After the drumming we begin to sing…then rattle. We are exposing the kidney to the healing vibrations of our instruments and voices. Soon that drum produces a certain tone and the beat takes on a certain cadence. Then I know it's beginning to work. We are affecting the patient. Now the sound will help break loose all that poison that's in there. That woman got well."

Steve explained that the woman suffering kidney problems had experienced severe trauma, abuse or molestation during her childhood. He said, "So what was first an emotional problem manifested physically," he said. "She stored her trauma in the kidney. Now she is older and can't control it anymore."

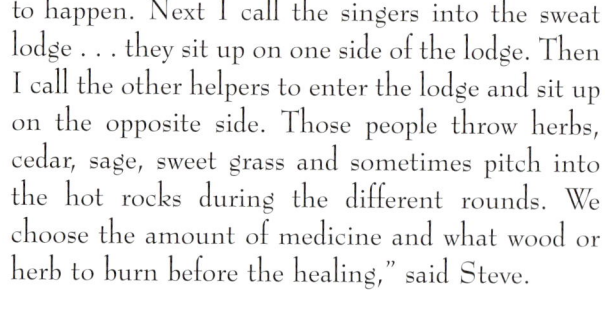

Steve Old Coyote carving a bird staff in his wood shop.

Tupile's youth enjoy an afternoon of traditional dance and music making.

entered the Colombian army and became an expert rifleman. In 1956, I returned to Panama and joined the National Guard. I trained people in jungle survival. To learn more about hospital care and clinical work, I went to the Brook Air Force Base to study at the Inter-American School. In 1962, I graduated as a clinical technician."

"How did you become a inatulele?" I asked. Simon answered, "Like many *curanderos* (healers), I had two *Maestros* (teachers) — my father, a inatulele, and néle, a seer. The prayers that I sing come from the néle. My father taught me about the plants," he said. But before Simon completed his apprenticeship, must never be separate from our work in healing," he said, staring into my eyes. He pointed his finger upward and paused for a moment. He sipped his beer in silence.

"Before we learn how to treat patients or collect the medicine, we must learn the healing songs and prayers," he said. "Without the songs the medicine will not be as effective. "I sing over plants that cure diarrhea, low red blood [cell] count, headaches and to help aggressive people control themselves."

Pregnant women can be helped when they are vomiting and dealing with morning sickness. Simon's treatments help women regain their

Simon Eliet, Ric Hajovsky and Pat Moffitt Cook discuss the applications of the inatulele (botanist's) shamanic songs.

ticeship, both maestros died.

The *saila* (chief) of Tupile was also a fine inatulele and accepted Simon as his student. "We spent hours in the jungle gathering *plantas medicinas*." Often when the saila was called away to other islands for political meetings, his patients would come to Simon for treatment. "Slowly I built up a reputation," he said. Rubbing his forehead, looking tired, he asked for a cold *cervesa* (beer).

As he sipped, he spoke: "I go to the jungle to find medicine for my patients. First I pray to *Dios* (God) to help me locate the plants I need. God appetites. "I treat people who drink too much. My medicine and song take away their desire to drink," he said.

"All the medicine is alive!" Simon said. He explained that the behavior of the inantulele is important. If the inatulele has done bad things then the medicine can turn bad and the patient can become more sick. "Like any good doctor I must be responsible to God and my patient. My song and intention to heal must be sincere," he explained.

Medicine that has been "sung over" will affect a better cure. The plants become more powerful.

CHAPTER SEVENTEEN

Simon Eliet
Inatulele from Panama

Simon Eliet was absent when our party of travellers and interpreters arrived on the Island of Tupile. Our Colombian and Kuna guides, Armenio and Leno, parked their motor-powered canoe alongside a wooden dock. Leno extended his hand to each of us, holding us steady as we climbed ashore. Everyone felt sticky from the salt water that had sprayed into the boat during the trip.

The sun and humidity had sapped our energy, forcing us to seek shelter. But shade was sparse, and hope for a cool glass of water, soda or iced beer looked bleak. We walked from one end of the tiny island to the other, searching. We saw beautiful robust babies playing outside cane huts, while their older siblings ran freely and laughed.

Many huts had adjacent gardens, brimming with vegetable greens. Women, sitting in doorways, waved as we passed. The men of the community were out fishing in small canoes; and everyone, including us, prayed for their success. Fish is the main staple on the island, and dinner depended on the day's catch.

We quickened our pace upon the incongruous sight of a Pepsi sign over a shop just ahead. *"Tienes Usted Pepsi?"* I asked. *"Si,"* replied the colorfully beaded Kuna woman standing beside a cooler. We collapsed on a bench, gulped our sodas, and rubbed the cold cans on our thighs, arms, cheeks and foreheads. This moment of peace would suffice until Simon Eliet, Tupilie's *inatulele* (botanist-chemist) returned.

SIMON ELIET, INATULELE

My flashlight began to flicker when the healer arrived. "I have just come from my patient's house," Simon explained. "I am on call twenty-four hours everyday. My wife knows I am here with you if I am needed."

Simon's sun-beaten face and kind brown eyes reflected his day's work. "I am past sixty years now," he said. "When I was fourteen, I went to Colombia to study different subjects in a school there. It was very difficult because I did not understand the language. I had no idea about terminology. It forced me to apply myself. At eighteen, I

Above: Simon Eliet

"Trauma can be stored in our nerves, stomach, and sometimes in the neck and head. People put trauma somewhere in themselves where we can deal with it at the time. It festers there and then grows worse over time. The first abuse damages us psychologically and spiritually and then slowly turns into a physical problem. Finally, this stored tension awakens; it becomes an active agent eating at us and spreading to other parts of our body," explained Steve.

The peyote songs send a therapeutic vibration to the mind and into the body of the ill; the pulse of the drum entrains the mind; the physical sound vibration penetrates the skin and damaged organ, finally shaking loose and changing the course of illness.

In other meetings, the roadman tells people to vocalize their thoughts and prayers during the second round of prayers: "I ask them to breathe and sing. This is like some kind of preventative health care. Doing this together in the sweat [lodge] releases potential damaging tension and energy from their bodies and minds.

> "I tell everyone to leave everything that is said here in the lodge. It's a safe place. Nobody is going to spread any gossip around once we leave. There needs to be trust and everybody must agree to that. We don't *do* healings here...we *are* healings here!" exclaimed the Roadman.

JAMES

A prevalent purpose of healing songs and prayers on the reservation is to support the tribe's young people. Steve's 21-year-old son James said, "Look around you. We live in a third world country right here in Washington. This reservation life is crazy, you know. All we have is each other and we gotta know that or we can't help each other."

This all-too-familiar story embodies a common theme for many indigenous societies that have experienced forced radical social change followed by economic hardship. Social trauma and disrespect create emotional and psychological pain and disorientation.

"All of us who are in this community hold a lot of respect for the sweat lodge meetings...for our elders' ways...and the Native American Church ways...and for that medicine, peyote," continues James. "Even though some young people get messed up out there, they can come here to the sweat, and sing with the roadman, and feel like themselves again. Our elders pray for us...they know we're going crazy, getting into drugs and alcohol. They take responsibility for us...singing the songs and making prayers every week for us young people. I'm learning this way from my Dad. I know all the songs. There are some guys my age who have a lot of responsibility in this church. The church makes us strong when we're in pain. If my brother or sister is hurting they can get healed here."

The songs that are sung in the meetings range from the use of vocables (phrases of linked vowels) to "Amazing Grace." Members of this church have faith that the "medicine" and songs used in the meeting will heal ailing bodies and minds. It also seems clear that most congregants cannot afford expensive health care. "We don't all have insurance, and a lot of us don't have good or steady paying jobs," Steve said.

"We sing because it feels good. We sing because it heals us. We sing out to the Creator who hears our songs and prayers. Singing is a good thing! AHO!"

Track 16 Steve Old Coyote
"Healing Songs for a Woman with Kidney Disease"
These three songs are used to treat illness in the Native American Church sweatlodge on the Suqamish Indian Reservation: Identifying the illness; Asking for the manifestation of healing and Giving thanks to the creator for listening. Sung by Steve Old Coyote and son James, accompanied by peyote rattle and iron pot drum. Recorded in September 1996.

They have a resin, sap or liquid in them; some bitter, red or white that becomes activated through the sound. "The medicine will work without the songs, but not as well," he said. "You must not separate these elements...that is simply the way."

"So your voice and song transfer an energy to the plant?" I asked. "No, *mira* Pat," he said. "Dios first made the inatuleles and then created the patients...and then created the plants. He told the plants, 'you're going to cure people.' The inatuleles were not created before everything, but before the plant medicine," Simon continued. "We are alive, like the plants. When the plantas medicinas hear the song, then they remember the job that God gave them in the beginning!"

SONGS

The inatulele chose three songs that evening. He explained that the songs are sung in the mountains over the medicine at the time of harvesting, before the plants are cut. The prayers can vary for the same illness depending on who they are intended for. Gender and age are deciding factors. "The song is the same; the only thing that changes is the name of the person," Simon said.

The first two songs Simon sang that evening were nearly identical. The first, for curing a little girl with fever (the wind way) was sung again for a pregnant woman suffering from fever. "I substitute the word *mujer* (woman) for *niña* (girl) . . . like that," he said. The last song was for a man with diarrhea caused by parasites.

"I sing in a shamanic language," Simon said. "The average person does not understand this. It is an old language. The song for curing diarrhea is saying, 'You have to cure the sick person. Remember the animals that suffer from this, dogs, parrots and goats . . . . we must understand their pain. We must combat this disease,' " Simon chanted.

"Right now I have ten patients on Tupile. One is suffering from anemia, another the mumps. Every day, I ask my patients if their symptoms have changed. If so, I change the medicine. So I am always thinking about my patients. If you want to be a inatulele you're going to suffer for it. I suffer headaches, hunger and mild jungle fever. But thank God, everything is going okay," he said, as he sat back and smiled.

Track 17
Simon Eliet
"Shamanic Chant for a Pregnant Woman with Fever"
The Inatulele (chemist) sings over botanical medicine to awaken it's healing properties. Recorded in Tupile off the coast of Panama in June 1996.

A traditional Kuna dance.

CHAPTER EIGHTEEN

Tibetan Oracle
Phawo Nyidhon

On clear mornings, the residents of Tashi Palkhiel village can see the distant summits of Annapurna and Macha-puchare. These sacred Himalayan mountains are revered in the various religious and social traditions that coexist in the surrounding areas. Their towering presence suggests that the gods watch over all living things.

Tashi Palkhiel village, outside of Pokara, Nepal, was established in 1959 as a Tibetan refugee camp. Tibetans from the Mount Kailas region, just north of the Nepalese border, fled their homeland — their land, cattle and extended families — to escape the torture and oppression of the Chinese invasion. Today, many of the village's residents work in carpet cooperatives and food stalls, spin wool for export and guide mountain treks.

> *"With their herds of yaks abandoned in Tibet, many of Tashi Palkheil's residents survive now by spinning wool shipped from Tibet and New Zealand. Others weave traditional Tibetan rugs for export to Katmandu and abroad."*
>
> Ian Baker,
> Field Associate for the
> Foundation for Shamanic Studies

Among the fleeing were Tibetan oracles. Several names have been used to identify these now-rare healers. *Phawo* or Tibetan shaman-oracle; *Lhapa* — the Tibetan term for shaman — literally, "a man of the gods"; and *nagpa lamas* and *nyen-jomo*, sorcerers and mediums.

"The phawo and nyen-jomos, male or female, are regarded by the Buddhists as typical representatives of *Bon*, the magico-religious belief of the Tibetan speaking people," according to Mircea Eliade, a pioneering scholar in Shamanic studies.

In 1986, the Dalai Lama invited oracle-healer Lhapa Wangchuk to Dharamsala, India. His Holiness bestowed upon Wangchuk the brocade ornaments of Tibet's previous State Oracle. "The shamanic forces of the mind and planet can be harnessed for the service of wisdom and compassion, each tradition enhanced by the perspectives and methods of the other," said His Holiness the Dalai Lama. This profound act of respect for Tibet's pre-

Above: The Himalayan Mountains